PRAISE FOR *THE GODLY KINGS OF JUDAH*

If you long to go deeper in the Word of God and discover hidden treasures, this is the book for you. Cynthia Cavanaugh has done an extraordinary job of making a study on *The Godly Kings of Judah* not only understandable, but intriguing and captivating. Her use of charts, applications, and the option to go beyond a surface knowledge of fascinating biblical leaders challenged me to be a faithful woman of influence for God's glory. I hope you'll dive into this well researched and profound resource and encourage a group of women to join you.

CAROL KENT
Speaker and author, *Becoming a Woman of Influence*

Cynthia Cavanaugh understands that many Christians struggle to make sense of all the kings in the Bible. She graciously, practically, and honestly helps anyone who desires to hear God's voice as she is confident that He is speaking to us through their stories. *The Godly Kings of Judah* will challenge you to obey like Jehoshaphat, to trust like Joash, to pray like Hezekiah, and to worship like Josiah.

DAVID T. LAMB
MacRae Professor of Old Testament, Dean of the Faculty, Missio Seminary
Author of *God Behaving Badly* and *1–2 Kings*

I long for my life to make a lasting impact. I want to live in a way that encourages my children, grandchildren, and others to cling passionately to Jesus. Cynthia Cavanaugh's new Bible study, *The Godly Kings of Judah*, offers solid biblical wisdom and practical help for anyone who desires to make an eternal difference and live a life that pleases God. In this engaging eight-week study, Cynthia not only makes ancient history exciting, she also shows its incredible relevance for our lives today. Your time with *The Godly Kings of Judah* is a wise investment with a valuable spiritual return.

KATHY HOWARD
Bible teacher and author of *Heirloom: Living and Leaving a Legacy of Faith*

Cynthia captivates you as she takes you on this fascinating journey of the life of kings and prophets in the Bible. *The Godly Kings of Judah* will set off a radical transformation in your life. More than historical factfinding, you will discover God's intentional sovereignty and power is equal to His grace, love, and forgiveness. So you want to discover God's mercy? It starts by living faithfully and engaging in the revolutionary book.

ROSALINDA RIVERA
Author, *Dare to Begin Again*
President of The Mercy House

For every woman who wrestles over her influence and impact, this study is a must. Cynthia teaches us how daily choices, a life of integrity, and faithful service to those around us create lasting legacies of faith of inestimable value. *The Godly Kings of Judah* spurs us on toward love and good deeds today that will change the lives of those we love for many more tomorrows.

ERICA WIGGENHORN
Author of *Letting God Be Enough: Why Striving Keeps You Stuck and How Surrender Sets You Free*

Cynthia is a student of the Word! Her expertise in helping others learn how to study God's Word comes through loud and clear in *The Godly Kings of Judah*. Your heart will be stirred and your passion ignited to leave a godly legacy to those coming up behind you. This is a great study!

BECKY HARLING
Conference speaker, coach, and author of *The Extraordinary Power of Praise*

If you want to grow as a woman of influence, this Bible study is for you. Cynthia Cavanaugh takes us on a journey of looking at the lives of Old Testament kings in a way that is relevant to our lives today. This study focuses on the faithfulness of God and the way He works in human lives through every generation.

DEBBIE ALSDORF
Author of *A Woman Who Trusts God*, *The Faith Dare*, and *Deeper*

THE
GODLY KINGS
OF JUDAH

FAITHFUL LIVING FOR
LASTING INFLUENCE

CYNTHIA CAVANAUGH

MOODY PUBLISHERS

CHICAGO

Edited by Amanda Cleary Eastep
Interior design: Kaylee Dunn
Cover design: Dean Renninger
Cover image of crown copyright © 2017 by Azuzl / iStock (879973430).
Interior illustration of Roman soldier copyright © 2017 by draco77 / iStock (845596310).
Interior illustration of doric column copyright © 2008 by aristotoo / iStock (165504815).
All rights reserved for all of the above images/illustrations.
Author photo: Jodi VanStraalen

ISBN: 978-0-8024-2174-6

Originally delivered by fleets of horse-drawn wagons, the affordable paperbacks from D. L. Moody's publishing house resourced the church and served everyday people. Now, after more than 125 years of publishing and ministry, Moody Publishers' mission remains the same—even if our delivery systems have changed a bit. For more information on other books (and resources) created from a biblical perspective, go to www.moodypublishers.com or write to:

Moody Publishers
820 N. LaSalle Boulevard
Chicago, IL 60610

1 3 5 7 9 10 8 6 4 2

Printed in the United States of America

I dedicate this book to my Aunt Trudy,
who faithfully lives her life for Jesus despite dark days and fierce storms.
Her joy is contagious and comes from a deep well of putting
God's Word at the center.
She is at the top among influencers in my life, teaching me that I am
never alone in the fire of life. God knows. He sees. He is enough.

Contents

AN INVITATION TO FAITHFUL LIVING

One of my favorite movies of all time is the Disney movie *National Treasure*.[1] It is a riveting adventure story of the Gates family searching for clues relating to their past that have remained hidden for generations. If they succeed in excavating the clues, they'll eventually be led to the truth of their heritage and the reward of a treasure.

In my love of history, I have been on a treasure hunt much like the Gates family. A few summers ago, I spent time reading through the books of 1 and 2 Kings and 1 and 2 Chronicles. God began to whisper significant lessons about the kings that were like stumbling onto the clues to a treasure. As I read and listened carefully, I began to chronicle the history of their lives and the era in which they lived. Themes began to emerge for me as I dusted off the clues. I began to see the importance of a life well lived.

Of the twenty kings of Judah and the nineteen kings of Israel, there were fewer than a handful who finished well. It troubled me to read of many who had all the favor and blessing of God only to find their unwise choices led them to reject God. Natural consequences followed their decisions with God's discipline. However, there was still His unfathomable mercy because of the faithfulness of previous generations.

In reflecting on my life, I began to see how easily I too could fall into the pattern of the kings and reject God's goodness. It made me take a hard look at myself and ask some tough questions:

What do I need to put in place right now to ensure I too won't fall into rejecting God in a season of my life?

What steps should I be taking now to prevent it?

How can I positively impact my family and friends and faithfully leave an intentional legacy?

Have I become too complacent? Do I settle for things that keep me from challenging myself and my relationship with God?

As I began to ponder these questions in depth, this study was born in order to explore the profound truths of what it takes to live out our days intentionally with faithfulness. In Week Two, we are introduced to the first of seven pillars of foundational truth that encourage us to live faithful lives. In the resource section at the back of the study, you will find the list of seven pillars that correspond with Weeks Two through Eight and a brief description of each for easy reference.

My prayer is that you will be challenged as we crack the vault of "secrets" in God's Word, and you will find your passion for living with the intention to impact your world and future generations for Christ.

How to Make the Most of This Study

Before we move to study the Bible lesson, I'd like to be your guide to help you get the most out of this study. We are tackling the books of 1 and 2 Kings and 1 and 2 Chronicles. These books are in the Bible, and they are considered what scholars would call historical narratives; they tell a story in history. In many ways, this study is like an archaeological dig because we will be uncovering clues and excavating truth to understand the story and how to apply God's truth to our life.

Whether or not you liked or loathed history from your school days, I hope to entice you on a journey to learn from these eight kings, with one addition. I've included a look at King Manasseh because of his dramatic repentance toward the end of his reign. If you follow the five steps below, you might discover that this digging into Scripture is precisely what you need!

1. PRAY — When you sit down to study, start with prayer. Ask God to open your eyes and give you the treasures of His Word as you learn. The Holy Spirit is your guide and will help you gain a heart of wisdom as you study.

2. READ THOUGHTFULLY — At times it can be tempting to think, "I know this story, so I am going to skip this one." But I don't want you to miss all that the Holy Spirit wants to share with you as you study His Word. Read thoughtfully and slowly, and have a highlighter and pen/pencil handy to make notes in the margins of your Bible.

At the beginning of each week, there will be a sizable chunk of the books of Kings and/or Chronicles to read. These readings are essential to providing the backdrop and the context for each week's lesson.

3. WRITING THE SCRIPTURE — Each week I'll ask you to handwrite sections of Scripture. Again, don't skip this part! I'll explain more later, but this is an integral part of embedding God's Word in your soul. Write, don't type.

4. MOVE AT YOUR OWN PACE — Yes, this study has a structure, but we all learn at different levels. Moving through this study is not a race or competition, and indeed, filling in all the blanks doesn't qualify you to be nominated as the next Bible study queen or theological scholar. I want to permit you to map out ahead of time how you will approach this study in your season of life.

If you are a mom of young kids, you probably don't have the luxury of sitting down during the day uninterrupted. You might be a single mom with a full-time job or you might be a full-time caregiver for an aging parent. Figure out what works for you, and then set the plan in motion. If you can decide *how* you will approach these next eight weeks instead of randomly thinking it will happen, you will be encouraged as you begin to study.

5. ARTIFACTS: DIGGING DEEPER SECTION — This is an optional study at the end of each week for those who want to spend a little more time reading and studying. Know and understand your limitations, and if you have the bandwidth, then go for it. If you can't, then no guilt, no shame.

Before you turn the page to Week One, write how you will approach this study. Be specific with days and times as much as possible. It doesn't mean you have to stick to it legalistically. This is your plan, your investment to grow in intimacy with Jesus as you study *The Godly Kings of Judah*.

Chronicles of the Kings Overview

SETTING THE STAGE

Faithfulness matters. *Your* faithfulness matters to God.

It doesn't matter to anyone as much as it does to your Creator. Redeemer. Restorer.

I often tell my leadership students at the university where I teach that it doesn't matter what you achieve or what you accomplish as a leader; what matters more is the type of person you choose to become. Our character and each thoughtful decision we make take us one step closer to a life of faithfulness, and our faithfulness, ultimately, affects our influence. Our influence determines our legacy, and our legacy speaks volumes about our faithfulness.

When I reflect on this, it scares me, frightens me to the core of my being. Who doesn't want to be counted faithful in this life? Who doesn't want to have a lasting positive influence? But how do we get to that place of God declaring us good and faithful servants and guaranteed lasting godly impact?

I am so glad you asked because I am offering you an invitation to walk with me down the halls of history in the books of Kings and Chronicles to find the silver thread among the kings of Judah who earned the statement by the writers, "And he did what was right in the eyes of the LORD." There were thirty-nine kings

between Israel and Judah, and only eight—yes, eight, or less than a quarter—were found to be faithful in God's eyes.

As we begin our study, I want you to think of yourself as an archaeologist, studying the lives of these ancient kings and uncovering clues that lead us to discover the secret of their faithfulness. We will examine the artifacts and see why these godly kings of Judah were set apart from all the other kings in Israel and Judah. Day Two of this week will introduce us to the four separate sections that we will refer to as we study.

Daily:

- *Survey* — digging out the truth from God's Word

- *Excavate* — an analysis and summary

- *Fieldnotes* — interpretation, what we've learned with questions; application for the day

Weekly:

- *Prayer* — a place for you to write a response to God in prayer, a truth, something that may have surprised you, a question, etc.

- *Artifacts: Digging Deeper* — a chance to dig a little deeper if you want to know more (no pressure, and remember: it's not extra credit for more stars in your crown!)

Are you ready? Put on your boots, pick up your tools, and let's get started!

THE BIG PICTURE

Do you enjoy learning the backstory of your favorite movie, novel, or place you are visiting? I've always been fascinated to discover the historical events that inspired the premise or setting of a movie or book, or the founding of a notable site. When my husband, Kevin, and I are exploring a new city or town, we often do some quick research on the exact spot we are visiting. Passing a landmark that looks interesting, Kevin may lean over and say, "Why don't you look that up?" And that begins our adventure of uncovering a clue.

Before we dive headfirst into learning about the godly kings of Judah, I want to take us on a historical overview to better understand the background and structure of the books of Kings. There is purpose and order to these two books, which will help us learn and grasp all that God desires to show us.

I recently took a course on the books of Kings and breathed a sigh of relief when the instructor affirmed that the books can be confusing for various reasons.[1] Sometimes you can't figure out who the author is talking about or which kingdom is referenced and in what time frame.

Our brief overview will set up the books to see where our eight godly kings fall in the combined forty-seven chapters of historical narrative and how the roles of other key players helped determine the legacy of these kings. These forty-seven chapters are divided into what is commonly known as 1 and 2 Kings, 1 Kings having twenty-two chapters, and 2 Kings having twenty-five chapters. In addition, we will cross-reference portions of the book of 2 Chronicles. Whereas the books of Kings is set up more like a historical narrative, the books of Chronicles add a perspective to the narrative in order to help the reader understand the spiritual implication of the events.[2] The author of the books of Chronicles also shows concern for faithfulness, temple worship and practice, prayer, and pointing the reader to God's character.

Let's talk about authorship. The books of Kings' author or authors are elusive. Some scholars think that Jeremiah was the author, which is consistent with the Talmud. Other scholars believe the author wrote the books in Judah where he would have had access to the national archives.[3] "Stylistically, Kings shares more connections to Deuteronomy than Jeremiah and since the book itself mentions no author, any conclusions about authorship must be considered speculative," states David Lamb in *The Historical Writings*. Lamb believes there might have been "multiple authors, scribes, editors, redactors, and perhaps even scribal communities."[4] Either way, because Kings is contained in the Bible, we know that it is God-breathed just like the rest of the books of the Bible.

To understand where our specific kings land in the overall picture, we first need to grasp the narrative of what happened after King Solomon's reign. Later in the week, we will explore what led to the demise of his reign. But for now, we just need to know that because of King Solomon's actions, the nation of Israel was divided into two kingdoms: the northern kingdom of Israel and the southern kingdom of Judah.

The forty-seven chapters of Kings 1 and 2 can be divided into three categories:

United Monarchy (Nation of Israel) — 1 Kings 1–11

Divided Kingdom — 1 Kings 12 through 2 Kings 17

Judah Alone — 2 Kings 17–25

All of the kings we will study were rulers of the southern kingdom of Judah, most of them reigning in the time frame of the divided kingdom. At the back of this book, you'll find The Kings Genealogy Timeline (with the exception of Solomon) you can use as a reference for these three time periods and all forty kings named in the books of Kings. Turn to that resource and highlight the kings we will be studying (listed below) to see the overall picture.

King Asa

King Jehoshaphat

King Joash (Jehoash)

King Amaziah

King Uzziah (Azariah)

King Jotham

King Hezekiah

King Manasseh

King Josiah

One of the other confusing elements of Kings is that two of these kings are referred to by different names in the books of Kings and books of Chronicles. (I've noted it next to their names above.) You will also notice as you look over these charts that some of the kings of Israel and the kings of Judah in the time of the divided kingdom also share the same, or similar, names. For example, King Jehoash of Israel starts his reign when King Jehoash (also called King Joash) reigns in Judah. Since we are only studying eight of the forty kings and they are all from the nation of Judah, that will be the context of our reading.

Trying to place the kings of Israel and Judah on an exact timeline can be a challenge. Judah and Israel used different systems to determine when the reign began, and it varied as the years passed. The two kingdoms also followed different calendars, and they began their calendars at different times, so the beginning of their years doesn't align either.[5] Clear as mud?

I hope this helps bring some clarity when you start reading the books of Kings and try to put the puzzle pieces together. If you are feeling a little confused, you are not alone! I am told that even scholars struggle with making it clear. We will stick to the context of Scripture that applies to each king and that should make it easier to understand.

We might think that the books of Kings are primarily about the rulers and their reign, but these books speak to the narrative about the character of God and His deep longing for the nations of Israel and Judah to follow Him in obedience. He is the central character and the focus of the books of Kings. The name YHWH is mentioned over five hundred times and God's name Elohim over two hundred times.[6] The messages from God were sent through the prophets, who also played a significant role in the season of the kings' reigns. God longed to bless them and help them flourish. But as we will learn, only a handful of kings decided to follow God with their whole heart while the others turned away and did what they determined was right in their own eyes.

To better understand this perspective, let's look at what we call the Judah Regnal Formula.[7] Are you with me? Not just the history lovers, I need all of you to stay with me; I promise this little nugget of information has a purpose, and you'll thank me later as you are reading.

The word regnal refers to "relating to a king or his reign."[8] Scripture outlines nine elements for each king of Judah. This is referred to as the Regnal Formula, although some information is available for a few kings. The northern kingdom has six similar regnal elements, but Judah adds a few extra. As we study the kings, you will fill in the blanks for the elements related to each king. For now, let's look at these elements and their descriptors.

Each of these elements helps serve a purpose and order for the books of Kings. Each creates structure and clarity. The book follows this structure not only for us to see the narrative but also to see the bigger picture from God's perspective.

Now the fun part. For each of our eight godly kings, read the corresponding verse and handwrite the verses in the space provided. Before I share the importance of being a scribe of Scripture, read Deuteronomy 17:18.

REGNAL FORMULA[9]

	ELEMENTS	DESCRIPTION
1	SYNCHRONISM	The date beginning the northern king's reign in relation to the southern ruler who is on the throne at the same time. For example, "In the seventh year of Jehu (of Israel), Jehoash (Joash) began to reign." (2 Kings 12:1)
2	ACCESSION AGE	How old the king was when he took the throne.
3	REIGN LENGTH	How many years, months, days, etc. he reigned.
4	MOTHER'S NAME	Name of king's mother and her relation or place of birth.
5	EVALUATION	From God's perspective...He did what was [_____] in the eyes of the Lord.
6	EXPLANATION	The narrative of his reign; what he did or didn't do.
7	HIGH PLACES/ NARRATIVE	Whether or not the high places were removed or others erected, and his contribution.
8	ANNALS REFERENCE	Usually, at the end of the narrative: "Are they not written in the book of the annals of . . .?"
9	DEATH NOTICE	If available, when and where he died and the cause of death.

Table modified from *The Historical Writings: Introducing Israel's Historical Narrative*. Used with permission.

What does God say in this passage concerning instruction for Israel's kings?

Wow! God is instructing them to write out a copy of the book of the Law for themselves. Why not have someone else do it? A king had his own scribes.

Now read all of chapter 17. *Notice what the following verses say, especially Deuteronomy 17:20, and write below the reason the kings were instructed to write a copy of the book of the Law.*

God knew that if the king would slow down and write each word out, he would be focused, and the living, breathing words of God would become embedded in his heart. Writing out Scripture helps us slow down, focus, and more importantly, retain what we read.

Are you ready to try it? Get your pens ready to record the following twenty-two verses and become a "scribe" of Scripture throughout the study!

Look up and then write out these verses in your notebook or journal:

King Asa — 1 Kings 15:9–11

King Jehoshaphat — 1 Kings 22:41–43

King Joash — 2 Kings 12:1–2

Amaziah — 2 Kings 14:1–3

Azariah — 2 Kings 15:1–3

Jotham — 2 Kings 15:32–35

Hezekiah — 2 Kings 18:1–3

Josiah — 2 Kings 22:1–2

How is your hand? A little worse for the wear? Shake it off; I have one last question for you to ponder. *What do you observe after writing the regnal elements in these verses? Any common threads?*

SOLOMON'S DECLINE

I must warn you upfront that the rest of this week might make your brain explode with details. As we set the stage for our study, I want to provide a broader overview of the backdrop for each king we will study. We will examine the divided kingdom, the role of prophets, and the role that enemies played in the nations of Judah, Israel, and the leaders. I promise, if you dig in deep with your archaeological tools, then the next several weeks will serve to set up the excavation site to find the secret to the godly faithfulness of our chosen kings. The reward of digging deep is finding patterns of truth you can apply to your life. These patterns can help you establish markers to remind yourself of God's faithfulness when you are tested through adversity.

Now that we had a quick overview yesterday of the kings, we need to look at the end of the reign of David's son Solomon and the beginning of the divided kingdom. Solomon's reign is the launching pad for understanding how Israel ended up having a northern kingdom, Israel, and a southern kingdom, Judah. This story is sobering, and there is much to uncover. As you read, make notes in the space provided (or in your journal) of any clues you might find concerning the decline of his reign.

Read 1 Kings 11:1–43.

After you've finished reading, make a list of all the reasons you find that point to Solomon's decline at the end of his reign.

Next, read 1 Kings 3:3–15 and 2 Chronicles 1:7–13 and contrast the characteristics of Solomon at the beginning of his reign and the end of his reign.

BEGINNING OF SOLOMON'S REIGN	END OF SOLOMON'S REIGN

Based on your observations in the chart, what changed between the beginning of Solomon's reign and the end of his reign?

What do you think Solomon could have done differently to stay on the path of faithfulness as did his father, King David?

Read 1 Kings 2:1–4. *What did David say to him? What did Solomon risk at the end of his reign, according to what his father told him?*

In 1 Kings 2:3, David urges Solomon "keep the charge of the LORD your God, walking in his ways and keeping his statutes, his commandments, his rules, and his testimonies."

The word *charge* in Hebrew means to "keep a watch," like a sentry to safeguard.[10] This implies Solomon's responsibility for the next generation and his influence.

In the same way, as believers, God calls us to keep the charge. Why? We may not be literal kings, but we are chosen, set apart by God to declare His glory.

Read 1 Peter 2:9. *What does this verse say about our role and position as believers?*

EXCAVATE

It's sad to read of all God gave Solomon and the success he experienced only to have it end tragically because of his idolatrous heart. In his book *Repentance: The*

Meaning & Practice of Teshuvah, Louis E. Newman gives us insight on the connection between sin and idolatry:

> Idolatry is pretending that something is divine and worthy of our devotion when, in fact, it is not. Sin and idolatry go hand in hand. Sin, we must conclude, is a kind of spiritual mistake, the result of being spiritually disoriented.[11]

We can conclude that Solomon indeed was spiritually disoriented, and it was the beginning of his demise and end of his reign over Israel.

Look again at the contrast between the beginning of Solomon's reign and the end. What do you think led to his biggest mistakes?

And what was his most significant loss in following his path?

FIELDNOTES

As I look over my family history, I see a significant contrast between my two grandmothers. One lived a life of suffering, and yet she made an intentional choice to lean in and trust God. As a result, her faithfulness still impacts my family and children to this day. We are living in the favor and blessing of my grandparents' faithful obedience. However, my other grandmother was determined to do what was right in her own eyes, choosing a life of alcohol that led to broken relationships. It had a destructive impact on her children.

A wall full of photographs at the top of the stairs reveals glimpses into the lives of these two grandmothers and our families. Every time I walk by, it is a stark reminder of which steps I want to follow to be counted faithful.

Now think about your family history. *Is there a place in your family tree where the contrast is similar? How has it impacted you and your family? What can you determine to do differently?*

THE DIVIDED KINGDOM

In Illinois on June 16, 1858, at the close of the Republican Convention, a famous speech was given by a man who quoted Mark 3:25 when he said: "A house divided against itself cannot stand." He went on to say, "I believe this government cannot endure permanently half slave and half free. I do not expect the Union to be dissolved—I do not expect the house to fall—but I do expect it will cease to be divided. It will become all one thing or all the other."[12]

We all recognize the familiar man in history who gave this speech and went on a few years later to be elected the sixteenth president of the United States, Abraham Lincoln. Whether or not his speech was inspired by the history of a divided biblical kingdom and Jesus' words, he was correct as the country was torn apart in the coming years, and the repercussions still exist to this day.

History often repeats itself, and if we take the time, we will see the plumb line that begins at the end of Solomon's reign. His sin led the nation of Israel to be severely divided and, years later, exiled as a result of the unrelenting disobedience of rulers and leaders.

Reading the books of Kings and the pleas of the prophets begging the people to turn back to God is heartbreaking. But before we go headlong into pointing a finger, we too need to examine our hearts and see where we tend to wander into temptation that leads to life-altering choices that have the potential to impact generations.

How did it happen that God's beloved people strayed so far away from God? Nearly all the kings, except for a handful, had the explanation and epitaph, so to speak, of being called evil.

One of King Solomon's primary mistakes was that he married foreign women, and "he clung to these in love" (1 Kings 11:2). His "wives turned his heart away after other gods" (1 Kings 11:4 NIV). What's more disturbing is that he left his worshiper's heart of Jehovah at the beginning of his reign only to exchange it for idolatry later in life. Now let's look at what happened after Solomon went off the deep end.

Before Solomon was led astray, he took up his father David's vision to build the temple. It was nearly five hundred years since Israel had left Egypt, and the people had no place to formally worship God. They gathered around the tent of meeting, and God's presence was embodied in the ark of the covenant. It's essential to recognize why the temple had such significance, and why in particular David wanted to be the one to accomplish this task. But God told David in 1 Chronicles 17 that he would not be the one to build it, but rather one of his sons.

In the ancient Near Eastern cultures, the importance of a temple represented the space where humans could interact with the divine. And in Israel's case, God set out particular terms for worship. The other significance was that the temple space was a place to celebrate feasts and festivals and served as a place for community, similar to how we would regard our church as a place of community.[13]

SURVEY

Read 1 Kings 6:1 and 2 Chronicles 3:1–17.

Imagine the temple in Jerusalem and its grandeur. From the description, what was it like?

Now read Solomon's benediction when the temple was dedicated in 1 Kings 8:54–61. What is the most important statement that Solomon makes in this passage? Does it evoke any emotions in you?

In Week One, Day Two, we read 1 Kings 11; reread verses 1–8. What is the explanation given for Solomon's behavior? Write it out in its entirety in your notebook or journal and let it sink in.

Read 1 Kings 11:9–13. *What was God's response to Solomon's actions?*

The wording in verse 11 in the English Standard Version (ESV) reads, "'Since this has been your practice and you have not kept my covenant and my statutes . . .'" Practice implies that Solomon's sin wasn't a one-time occurrence. Practice means repetition, and unfortunately, Solomon refused to give up the practice of spiritual adultery. The New International Version (NIV) reads, "'Since this is your attitude and you have not kept my covenant and my decrees. . . .'"

I love and appreciate the way the New Living Translation (NLT) gives God's account of His anger toward Solomon:

The LORD was very angry with Solomon, for his heart had turned away from the LORD, the God of Israel, who had appeared to him twice. He had warned Solomon specifically about worshiping other gods, but Solomon did not listen to the LORD's command. So now the LORD said to him, "Since you have not kept my covenant and have disobeyed my decrees, I will surely tear the kingdom away from you and give it to one of your servants. But for the sake of your father, David, I will not do this while you are still alive. I will take the kingdom away from your son. And even so, I will not take away the entire kingdom; I will let him be king of one tribe, for the sake of my servant David and for the sake of Jerusalem, my chosen city." (1 Kings 11:9–13 NLT)

In other words, God is saying, since this is who you are, i.e., in practice and attitude, *you*, Solomon, have done this (as the NKJV translates). Solomon committed this sin by himself because he disregarded what God said about marrying foreign women and worshiping idols. It is a sad commentary of willful disobedience on Solomon's part, and the consequences were felt for generations to come.

Does this mean that the several hundred years that followed were years of waste and desolation? What do you think?

Read the following verses. *What does each tell you about God?*

Isaiah 30:18

Deuteronomy 4:31

Luke 1:50

Though this is a very dark part of the story, we can see over and over again how God longs to be merciful to those who fear Him. In turn, when we have a healthy fear of God, we have hope to make good choices to follow Him in obedience.

The events that take place after Solomon's reign are a convoluted part of the story regarding how the kingdom became divided. Now hang with me, and we will start to put the puzzle together to see the bigger picture. When God spoke to Solomon and said He wouldn't tear away the whole kingdom but leave one tribe, God was referring to the tribe of Judah. Hence, the future kings reigned over the southern kingdom and are referred to as the southern kingdom of Judah. This is where the Davidic line continued for the promised coming Messiah, Jesus.

As part of the consequence of Solomon's sin, God incited three adversaries against Solomon who would help fulfill the prophecy of the divided kingdom. One of these adversaries was his servant Jeroboam, the son of Nebat, an Ephraimite of Zeredah. The northern kingdom represented the ten tribes given by God to Jeroboam. God gave to Solomon's son Rehoboam one tribe, the tribe of Judah, and he became the first king of the southern kingdom.

Let's explore the details of what incited the division.

Read the story of Jeroboam in 1 Kings 11:26–38. *What is God offering Jeroboam? What are the criteria God requires for Jeroboam to keep the throne?*

The other interesting thing we want to note here is that the prophet Ahijah the Shilonite enters the story to give Jeroboam a message.

Why do you think he delivered the message the way he did?

Because Solomon's house is threatened, he sets out to destroy Jeroboam, even though God told Solomon that He would tear the kingdom away from him and give it to one of his servants. After Solomon gets word of the message from the prophet Ahijah the Shilonite to Jeroboam, he tries to kill him. Jeroboam flees to Egypt and stays under the protection of Shishak, king of Egypt, until Solomon's death.

In the next part of the story, we find Solomon's son Rehoboam on the throne.

Read what happens in 1 Kings 12:1–15. *Note verse 15; what do we discover about this turn of events?*

EXCAVATE

The story's climax occurs in 1 Kings 12:16–24. There we discover how the kingdom finally becomes divided into north and south. Ten tribes make up the northern kingdom, and Judah (including Benjamin), makes up the southern kingdom. The geographic setting of each kingdom was vastly different, and that impacted the way the kings carried out the business of the day.

The ten northern tribes of Israel were spread out across a diverse fertile region from Galilee to Samaria. This left them open to foreign invasion and a more significant cultural influence because they were spread out geographically and near neighboring nations.

In contrast, Judah, the southern kingdom, was "confined to the central hill country and was bordered by desert regions to the south and the east."[14] The seat, or capital, of Judah was Jerusalem; the northern kingdom, however, established its center and capital in the city of Shechem, in the hill country of Ephraim (its capital later changed to Samaria). For a more visual picture, look at the map of the northern and southern kingdoms at the back of the book.

Jeroboam's downfall was this: he had a greater fear of people than of God, and it led him to create his own religious system.

As I reflect on Jeroboam's reign and the beginning of the many years of spiritual waste and destruction of the northern kingdom, I consider how often we fall into the trap of taking matters into our own hands because our fear of others leads us away from trusting God for the outcome. Ouch! Am I ever guilty of this!

Can you think of a time that you took matters into your own hands? Explain.

When we follow our own path, God allows events to occur in order to accomplish His purpose in spite of our choices. This isn't the best path, but God still has the last word in the design of His plan.

At this point in our study, we find the kingdom divided because of sin. The consequences of sin had significant generational impact as we are about to discover over the next several weeks.

Consider the answer you wrote in the Excavate section. When you followed your own path, did things turn out the way you'd hoped? Why or why not?

Prophets and Voices of Wisdom

How many times have you had someone say to you, "The Lord told me to tell you . . ."? When that happens to me, I have my doubts, unless it is someone I trust. When I was pregnant with our third child, we already had two little boys and were excited for another addition to our family. One Sunday, someone came up to me after church and casually shared with me that God told them that this next child was going to be a girl. They were so certain. And wouldn't you know it, on a spring day in April, Jason was born. We couldn't have been more thrilled to have three boys.

We all need a voice of wisdom in our life, but not the kind that says God "told me," assuming to be the voice of God. Jehovah made sure that the kings received His messages through the prophets, His messengers chosen and called by Him.

It's important that we consider the significance of the prophets who came alongside the kings of Judah. They were not only appointed by God to be His "voice," they were also the voice of reason and wisdom for the leaders of the day. As we study each king, we will read the specific messages of these prophets in Scripture. But first, let's look more carefully at the purpose of the prophets in the books of Kings.

In many ways, the prophets could be seen as the heroes in the story of the kings. They were the voices of wisdom acting on behalf of God. They had incredible influence and delivered good news, dire news, warnings, and judgments to the leaders.

There are three terms in the Bible used in reference to the word "prophet." (For those of you who enjoy stats, you will love this little bit of information.) The first comes from the Hebrew word *nabi*, which occurs a total of 317 times in the Old Testament, including eighty-four times in the books of Kings. The book of Jeremiah contains the most with ninety-five, with Kings coming in second. The next term, "man of God," or *ish Elohim*, is referenced fifty-one times with seventy times total in the Hebrew Bible. The last is the word "seer," which appears once in 2 Kings 17:13. Otherwise, the prophets are referenced by proper names, sometimes anonymously, or in groups.[15]

SURVEY

There are also three types of messages delivered primarily to rulers: counsel, prediction, and judgment.[16] Let's break these down.

Read each verse. In the first column, write in the name or term by which the prophet is referenced. In the second column, fill in the type of message the prophet delivered to the king, i.e., were they words of counsel, words that predicted an event or outcome, or words of judgment? In the third column, note each king's response.

SCRIPTURE	PROPHET TERM	MESSAGE CATEGORY	RESPONSE
1 KINGS 12:22–24			
1 KINGS 14:2, 5–12			
1 KINGS 17:1			

These prophets in and of themselves didn't possess any power; instead, they represented Yahweh, and because their voice was the voice of God, they played a significant role in the lives of these kings in the kingdoms of Judah and Israel.

EXCAVATE

Besides bringing messages to the kings and the nations the kings ruled, prophets also fulfilled another role: God gave them the ability to bring healing and life . . . or death.

Read the passages below. *What do you discover in these Scriptures about the prophets' messages, the consequences of not heeding the prophet's message, and/or the actions of the people who listened to the prophets' words?*

1 Kings 17:8–16

1 Kings 17:17, 22–23

2 Kings 1:9–17

FIELDNOTES

As you can see, the prophets played a considerable role in the books of Kings.

Do you have a voice of wisdom in your life to help hold you accountable? How does this person hold you to account?

THE CAPTIVITY OF ISRAEL AND JUDAH

You did it! You made it through the nitty-gritty digging. You are a biblical archaeologist! I have one last task for us this week.

This week's study took me the longest to write. I spent months in research. I marinated, reflected, took walks, and contemplated each and every word on these pages. My dining room table was littered with every book I could find on the kings, commentaries, and Bible translations . . . and snacks of every sort, from salty chips to chocolate!

Why? Because being a disciple of God's Word is crucial if we are to appreciate God's character and who He is. The Bible isn't just stories and methods and formulas to help us live righteously; its lessons and challenges help us live faithful lives that have a lasting influence.

There is one little catch to living a faithful life. Just like the biblical kings and the people they ruled, we too are human. We are tempted and influenced by the culture around us. And enemies? Do we ever have enemies! Maybe not flesh and blood enemies with swords threatening to conquer our neighborhoods and towns, but enemies that subtly insinuate themselves into our lives in order to derail us from living faithfully.

So, besides understanding the historical overview, the divided kingdom, and the roles of the kings and the prophets, we need to understand who Judah's enemies were and how they influenced their ability to be and remain faithful. If the prophets were the "real heroes" communicating on behalf of God in the books of Kings,[17] then the surrounding nations were the enemies that presented a temptation to the kings and the nations' future.

SURVEY

Read the verses in the Scripture column that correspond to the king listed in the first column. In the third column, name the enemy nation listed in the Scripture. In the last column, write out what danger the enemies' influence posed and the kings' vulnerable position.

NAME OF KING	SCRIPTURE	JUDAH'S ENEMY	DANGER OF THE ENEMY'S INFLUENCE
ASA	1 Kings 15:16–22		
JEHOSHAPHAT	2 Chronicles 20		
JOASH	2 Kings 12:17, 18		
AMAZIAH	2 Kings 14:1–14		
UZZIAH	2 Chronicles 26:6–8		
JOTHAM	2 Chronicles 27:4–7		
HEZEKIAH	2 Kings 18–19		
MANASSEH	2 Chronicles 33:10–13		
JOSIAH	2 Kings 23:28–30		

EXCAVATE

You've done a ton of hard work this week. I hope you have an overview of where we are headed in the days and weeks ahead.

Write down three facts you've learned about the history of the kings and/or Judah or Israel that you didn't know before.

FIELDNOTES

As we finish the first week, write a prayer expressing to God what you learned and what you hope to learn over the next several weeks. Share it with your Bible study group or a friend and ask them to pray for you.

PRAYER

Dear God . . .

Exploring Family History

Interestingly, in 2 Chronicles, there is no mention that God was angry with Solomon for his spiritual adultery and turning away from the Lord as outlined in the books of Kings. The author of Chronicles likewise didn't include David's sin with Bathsheba but instead focused on the Lord's promise and fulfillment of the Davidic line. Why were these details left out? Primarily because the purpose of the book of Chronicles is to encourage the generations and focus on the faithfulness of God. The author does not necessarily avoid these details but perhaps assumes the reader already knows them.[18]

How many times have I listened to the history of a family, but the details of negative behaviors are left out while the positive is emphasized, overshadowing the consequences of mistakes and failures? More times than I can count. Not to fault the author of Chronicles in his assessment of David and Solomon, but I think it is important to explore our history so we don't repeat the sins of the past generations. And yet, settling on the sovereignty of God and the choices of our families also helps us to see the bigger picture of the impact their influence may have on our lives.

Review the Survey section in Day One. What do you see as the main differences between David and Solomon?

Where do you see God's grace and faithfulness in the account of their lives?

King Asa and King Jehoshaphat

REVIVING OBEDIENCE

Asa — Healing or Cure[1]

Asa did what was right in the eyes of the LORD,
as David his father had done.
1 KINGS 15:11

Jehoshaphat — Jehovah has judged[2]

He walked in all the way of Asa his father. He did not turn aside from it,
doing what was right in the sight of the LORD.
1 KINGS 22:43

We don't hear the word *revival* tossed around much these days. In the mid-nineteenth century revival meetings were common. Economic downfall before and after the Civil War in the 1860s brought hardship. Despair ran rampant. People were beyond discouraged at the state of events in the country. Does that sound familiar today?

Ordinary people who loved Jesus, like you and me, began organizing prayer meetings. The meetings started popping up in towns and cities across America.

In New York City alone, after banks were failing and the stock market crashed, these events triggered more than 10,000 people gathering daily for prayer. Revival meetings filled to overflowing with people crying out to God in desperate times. These meetings were considered a place where God showed up in ways out of the ordinary Sunday church service. The stories of transformation and answered prayer spread like wildfire, jumping oceans to spread across countries such as Scotland, England, Wales, Ireland, and beyond. God was on the move, and it changed generations of Christians.[3]

Here we find Israel in a place similar to the one we studied in Week One. A kingdom divided after Solomon—stripped of wealth by foreign nations, unrest, oppression, and enemies pressing in on every side. Two successive kings, descendants of David and Solomon, father and son, Rehoboam and Abijam, do little to help the situation. They are bent on practicing evil and turning Judah over to destruction. After Abijam's death, there is a crack of light in the darkness of leadership. Along comes Solomon's great-grandson, Asa, who is crowned king after his father's reign of just three years. We see hope for reforms in a new direction—a changing of the guard, bringing revival to Judah. Asa is the first of the four reforming rulers in Judah, the other three being Joash, Hezekiah, and Josiah.

God says this of Asa in 1 Kings 15:11: "Asa did what was right in the eyes of the Lord, as David his father had done." Maybe Asa learned from watching his father and grandfather and discovered the clues left by the legacy of his great-great-grandfather, King David, that the only way back to God is through the obedience of revival to restore the legacy.

GRANDMOTHERS

When we talk about obedience I immediately think about the first word my children spoke, NO! As they developed their vocabulary, it didn't matter what the question was because no was the most frequent answer. When trying to steer them to obey, their initial response to their mom was to say no. They soon learned it was better to say yes and be obedient rather than risk the consequences for their behavior.

I am hoping that you have a wholehearted yes to learning about our first godly king Asa, and how his obedience changed the cultural landscape of Judah. We are going to dig right in this week and use our masterful tools to not only extract the truth we find in God's Word but also lay the first of **seven pillars** we will discover in this study that will help us live faithful lives and leave a lasting influence. Our first pillar is *Reviving Obedience*. At the back of the book, you can find a page that lists all seven pillars and brief summaries of each.

SURVEY

Read 1 Kings 15:8–24 and 2 Chronicles 14–16.

Now let's begin to unearth the clues to discover revival in our lives.

You are going to fill in a Regnal Chart for each king, with observations. I'll fill in this first one to help you begin, and you may also refer back to the Regnal Formula chart in Week One, Day One for the descriptors of each element. Feel free to add any other observations you might find in the evaluation and narrative material sections from your earlier reading.

JUDAH REGNAL FORMULA: KING ASA

	ELEMENTS	ASA OF JUDAH: 1 KINGS 15:8–24 AND 2 CHRONICLES 14–16
1	SYNCHRONISM	In the 20th year of Jeroboam, king of Israel
2	ACCESSION AGE	Not mentioned
3	REIGN LENGTH	41 years
4	MOTHER'S NAME	Maacah (in this instance his mother isn't listed but this is his grandmother)
5	EVALUATION	"He did what was right in the eyes of the LORD, as David his father had done." 1 Kings 15:11
6	HIGH PLACES	Asa removed all the idols his fathers had made, but didn't remove the high places
7	NARRATIVE MATERIAL	He removed his grandmother from being queen mother because she made an image of an idol; he restored the altar of the LORD, made a covenant with all the people to seek the LORD, brought into the house of God things that his father had dedicated. (2 Chr. 15)
8	ANNALS REFERENCE	1 Kings 15:23: "The rest of all the acts of Asa, all his might, and all that he did, and the cities that he built, are they not written . . ."
9	DEATH NOTICE	He was buried with his father in the city of David his father. Jehoshaphat reigned in his place. 1 Kings 15:24

If you could choose one phrase to describe King Asa's reign, what would it be?

What are some of King Asa's characteristics?

What were some of King Asa's reforms?

What was the cost to Asa's family in carrying out the reforms? (1 Kings 15:13)

Why is removing his grandmother significant?

Read Exodus 20:3–6. *What does God say about idols? Why is it important to follow this command?*

As I shared in Week One, my two grandmothers were as opposite as night and day. One left a legacy of truth and love in Jesus, and the other left a path of brokenness and hurt caused by alcohol abuse. I never knew the grandmother who chose the path of addiction because she died when I was a toddler. But by God's grace, my dad chose a legacy his children want to follow and reversed the destruction. The key word here is "chose."

Dad decided to follow Jesus hard and fast when I was a teenager and not let his past define his future or the future of his family. I am grateful to my dad for his choice, although I know his painful past threatened to influence his legacy. He brought spiritual revival to our family through his intentional decision to turn away from the path his parents modeled.

Scripture doesn't tell us of the relationship between Asa and his grandmother. We can only speculate the difficulty for King Asa to remove her from her position and strip her of her title. At the very least, there may have been other family members or palace attendants who frowned on his decision. We don't know, but let's say she went kicking and screaming, which would have made it more difficult for King Asa.

What does this significant choice reveal about his devotion to God?

It's easy to blame unruly family members in our family tree for our behavior and it's hard to instead choose obedience in order to break the chain and invite revival. We might smile, almost boasting, and say, "Yes, I have a quick temper because I am Irish, and we Irish have been feisty for generations; it's just the nature of who we are." Or, "Don't you know that all Germans are stubborn?" Or, "Our grandfather says that what makes us strong is our _____." Then you can fill in the blank with whatever has been adopted as acceptable.

Revival doesn't come without repentance and the obedience to cause a major paradigm shift in the generational sin pattern. Just as Asa had to take a sobering look at his family and courageously make changes, we too can't excuse generations of attitudes and behaviors if we want to invite revival into our life to change the future. We can, with the Holy Spirit's help, remove attitudes and behaviors that have been entrenched for so long in our family that they are seen as "normal." If we are going to seek revival, we have to investigate those places in our lives that for generations may have become strongholds and held us back from pursuing God with our whole hearts.

Where does revival need to happen in your life?

Is there anyone in your family tree whose influence or sin patterns have created a struggle for you to follow God with your whole heart?

How can you wisely protect your heart from allowing their influence to keep you from obeying God in revival? Take a few minutes and pray for them, asking God to bring restoration to their heart.

As we finish up today's lesson, review the chart about King Asa. Is there any specific phrase or Scripture that resonates?

REMOVING THE HIGH PLACES

When I visited Cambodia several years ago, it wrecked my heart. I've seen poverty on many levels but never the combination of both physical and spiritual poverty. It was horrific as I drove through the filthy, smoke-filled city streets witnessing religious practices of idol worship that only intensifies the cycle of unimaginable poverty.

Little children hungry and dirty, soliciting despicable acts for adults, the evidence of human trafficking behind dark torn curtains. On every hill or mountain is a temple set up for the worship of a false god. They rose over the city and the villages we visited; the spiritual darkness suffocated my spirit. I then understood the meaning of high places from Scripture and realized that I too have my high places. They may not be stone and mortar sitting on top of a hill. They are people and things I put in place of God—human devices that create unrest and oppression, robbing my peace. They tempt me away from being obedient and pursuing revival, from making the right decision to choose a godly life and legacy.

High places. We all have them. And just as God asked Judah and Israel to tear them down, He asks us to do the same, and for one reason: so we can experience revival in our soul and worship Him alone. Revival keeps us soft and tender to the voice of Jesus and brings peace. Revival brings healing to our relationships and changes the landscape of the generations.

SURVEY

Read Deuteronomy 6:1–9 and Deuteronomy 12:1–14.

The high places in the Bible were places of worship with shrines where people could practice all forms of evil rituals. God had forbidden His people to engage in these practices.

Before we look at what God says about high places, list God's specific instructions to His people in Deuteronomy 6:1–9.

What are the primary reasons that God says these instructions are so important?

Who were these instructions to be passed down to? Why?

Now let's look at Deuteronomy 12:1–14. List the steps God outlined for removing the high places and for worshiping Him.

STEPS TO REMOVE THE HIGH PLACES	STEPS TO WORSHIP GOD

Read 2 Chronicles 14:2–5. *What is the progression of steps that Asa followed that brought peace to the kingdom of Judah?*

How is the order of what happened important in these verses?

Do you recognize any high places in your life? If so, write about them here.

Are you missing joy and peace? How might you experience revival in your heart?

In your family and among those in your sphere of influence, who has the most to gain when you seek to follow God's heart in revival by removing your high places? Why?

EXCAVATE

I have to confess, the older I get, the consequences of not being obedient scare me to death! As I read about the kings of Judah, so many of them didn't follow through with their whole hearts. It is easy to look at their life and point a finger as to the reasons why. The observation that sticks with me as I read the account of the kings is that many obeyed God, but only half-heartedly. They still kept the high places, and that decision became a snare to the nation they were leading. Many times, this happened as a result of acquiring more wealth and success. They became dependent on their resources rather than God.

This was true of King Asa: "The high places were not taken away. Nevertheless, the heart of Asa was wholly true to the LORD all his days" (1 Kings 15:14). God, in His mercy, still gives this account of Asa about his heart being with Him. But not removing the high places had implications for the generations to come, and we will see that later in our study as we read about the end of King Asa's life.

I can be stubborn, just like King Asa, with the habits I've erected and justified, thinking they won't hurt anything or anybody. And yet I want my family and friends to say my heart too was completely with the Lord my entire life, including tearing down my high places.

What if we work hard to go further, so the generations watching and following don't become trapped by our high places? Sobering thought, don't you think?

Find a quiet place and take a few minutes to write a prayer listing your high places. (See the description of a high place in this week's Artifacts: Digging Deeper section if you need more definitions.)

Ask God to help you tear down the high places and replace those areas with obedience so you can open the door to revival. It is always helpful when removing sin in our life to replace it with a verse of Scripture. God's Word brings revival.

FIELDNOTES

Can you tell I like charts?

In the chart, list your high places. Fill in the second column with a verse or verses that you can pray to help you begin to tear that high place down. Finally, jot down an action step for obeying. I've given you an example of a high place that I've asked God to help me conquer.

MY HIGH PLACE	SCRIPTURE TO PRAY OVER	MY ACTION PLAN
EXAMPLE: Trying to win others' approval to appear perfect and without failure.	"For we are his workmanship, created in Christ Jesus for good works, which God prepared beforehand, that we should walk in them." (Eph. 2:10)	Take a step back and ask myself, "What is my motive for gaining approval in this situation?" Stop and ask Jesus to help me in the moment.

For the next seven days, make a commitment to review each verse you chose to cover the high place you want removed. Review your plan when you are tempted to rebuild the high place. Ask God for a prayer of covering for the next generation that, because of your example, they will see nothing can keep them from depending on God with wholehearted obedience.

This is challenging work we've done in our study today, and I am so proud of you for taking the time to listen to God and soak in His Word! We may not see the payoff immediately, but I trust the generations that follow will thank us for our faithful commitment to be wholly dependent on God in worship.

My maternal grandmother was faithful and true to Jesus. She was not perfect by any means, and even with Alzheimer's disease dimming her mind, she cried out to God in songs and Scripture until her death. She had a fortified plan, and when her mind betrayed her body, the altar where she worshiped her whole life rose above. There isn't a week that goes by that her influence doesn't impact my life.

As we finish up today, read 2 Chronicles 15:1–4 aloud. In the space below, write the phrase you found to have the most impact.

THE HEART OF REVIVAL

Emma Dryer was a woman in the nineteenth century who lived a quiet and safe life dedicated to God but not necessarily entirely devoted to Him until deep trials came into her life. She enjoyed life as the head instructor at Illinois State University, training young women to be teachers. She became severely ill with typhoid fever, which was raging in the United States in the mid-1800s. Emma was not used to being inactive, and while lying on her sickbed fighting a fever, she asked God for a second chance to serve Him intentionally. God's Word brought fresh understanding as to His purposes and plans. God did heal her, and this was the spark that lit Emma's heart on fire to serve a dying world.

After recovering from her illness, she visited friends in Chicago. Through a series of events, including the Great Chicago Fire, God revealed her assignment to her. Her heart was drawn to the wayward women who had recently arrived in the city. Many, single like Emma, took work as prostitutes and barmaids. Emma was determined to help these women and others and knew God would guide her. Her goal was to "get a Bible into the hand of every woman in the city and train them to lead Bible studies of their own."[4] She wanted them to know how to lead devotions in their own families.

Emma met and worked with D. L. Moody, joining him in establishing what would become Moody Bible Institute. Emma was passionate about the Bible and wanted to train up as many men and women as possible to seek revival to understand God's Word and His truth.[5]

This story reminds me how we can love God, as Emma did before her illness, and even serve Him but without embracing wholehearted commitment. Instead, we play it safe and trust God only as far as our "safety net" extends. Emma's life is such an example of becoming more devoted through trials and serving Him faithfully until the end.

I want to spend our time today talking about what true obedience and revival look like. We read about King Asa and his determination to deconstruct what his previous family rulers had built on total spiritual adultery. King Abijam, Asa's father, even talked the talk when he went up in battle against King Jeroboam, taunting him. Second Chronicles 13 tells the battle story and how God gave King Abijam victory because "they cried out to the Lord" for help (2 Chron. 13:14).

Yet, in the books of Kings, we see God's final verdict of King Abijam. Sadly, he walked in all the ways of the sins of his father Rehoboam and his grandfather Solomon. We are told that his heart wasn't wholly true to Yahweh (1 Kings 15:3). Along with his father, he is listed as one of the evil kings, except for this single victory in Chronicles. His obedience didn't last; there was no revival.

SURVEY

Read 2 Chronicles 15:1–12.

Write out 2 Chronicles 15:1–7 in your notebook or journal.

What can we discover in these verses about the requirements for true revival?

Reread 2 Chronicles 15:8–11. *What did Asa do as a result of the prophet Azariah's message?*

Write out verse 12 word for word.

What does it look like for us to seek God with all our heart and our soul? What does that look like for you today, tomorrow, and this coming week? Be specific. Don't rush an answer to just fill in the blank. You might want to think about it for a while and come back and write it down.

EXCAVATE

Three things precede true revival that we can learn from this story in 2 Chronicles. Use the tools you've acquired to dig them out.

1. 2 Chronicles 15:2 _____

2. 2 Chronicles 15:4 _____

3. 2 Chronicles 15:8 _____

Let's see if we came up with a match.

1. The first thing that precedes revival is: we have to be looking for one. And that means seeking God and listening to His voice. This is what King Asa did, and he listened to the prophet Azariah (not to be confused with King Azariah) because Asa had the heart to follow God (v. 8). When we seek God, He promises He will find us!

2. The second thing that precedes revival is: we have to turn to Him no matter what. As the passage implies, when we are in distress, we must surrender to God and not try to figure out our dire situation all by ourselves. This was the downfall of many of the kings and even Asa at the end of his reign. Whether he forgot or was too confident in his success, we don't know. But no matter what, in all things and at all times, we must surrender.

For example, Asa made a grave error in 2 Chronicles 16:1–10 by trusting his wealth and the king of Syria to protect him from the king of Israel, Baasha. As a result, he received a visit from Hanani, the seer who rebuked Asa's action of depending on King Aram of Syria rather than God. King Asa became angry, threw the seer in prison, and didn't heed God's message sent by Hanani nor accept the consequences of his sin.

The author of Chronicles ends his account of Asa's reign right there, and the king who started well finished foolishly all because of this one act. However, I would venture to say that there was a culmination of many small decisions. These decisions may not have been significant in themselves and may even have appeared harmless, but they may have led Asa to take matters into his own hands and decide what was best.

3. The third and last precedent for a revival is: we have to be obedient and walk out that obedience. In other words, we need to act. Note what Asa does in 2 Chronicles 15:8: "He took courage and put away the detestable idols." And he "repaired the altar of the LORD."

The word courage in this passage is the Hebrew word *chazaq* and means "to fasten upon, seize, be strong, fortify."[6] Asa needed courage and lots of it! If we remember, his father Abijam did the opposite and rode the cultural tide of idolatry. For Asa, doing something meant going against the people his father had reigned over, not to mention his father (and the precedent set by his grandfather and his great-grandfather Solomon). They were comfortable with idolatry, and all of Israel and Judah worshiped idols. Asa was the first ruler to change the spiritual climate in generations. God sent Azariah to encourage Asa and also give him a message of hope and challenge: "The LORD is with you while you are with him. If you seek him, he will be found by you, but if you forsake him, he will forsake you" (2 Chron. 15:2).

Is this you? Are you the first in generations to take a stand to love the Lord your God, breaking the chains of sin and bondage in your family? Take courage, fasten yourself to the Lord like Asa did, and do what you need to do to preserve the generations that follow. Your godly influence can last for eternity.

FIELDNOTES

Psalm 19:7 confirms what is necessary for our lives for revival in our souls: "The law of the LORD is perfect, reviving the soul; the testimony of the LORD is sure, making wise the simple." Just like the kings of Judah, listening to God's Word is the glue to faithful and lasting influence.

Read Psalm 19:7 aloud and then write it out word for word.

Take a few minutes to stop and thank God for His faithfulness in your life and renew your courage to do the same as Asa did to create a faithful legacy.

TELLING THE TRUTH

The courage that Asa displayed left a mark on his son, the next king of Judah, Jehoshaphat. In the books of Kings, there are only a few verses dedicated to the mention of Jehoshaphat, and the narrative changes for the several following chapters. The focus is on the northern kingdom and its rulers. At the end of 1 Kings 22, the regnal formula is given.

Now you get the chance to complete your first regnal formula on your own for King Jehoshaphat.

Reread 1 Kings 22:41–44 and read 2 Chronicles 17:1–6.

JUDAH REGNAL FORMULA: KING JEHOSHAPHAT

	ELEMENTS	JEHOSHAPHAT OF JUDAH: 1 KINGS 22:41–50; 2 CHRONICLES 17–20
1	SYNCHRONISM	In the 4th year of Ahab, king of Israel
2	ACCESSION AGE	
3	REIGN LENGTH	
4	MOTHER'S NAME	
5	EVALUATION	
6	HIGH PLACES	
7	NARRATIVE MATERIAL	
8	ANNALS REFERENCE	
9	DEATH NOTICE	

Read 2 Chronicles 17:3–6.

In the opening explanation of Jehoshaphat's reign, we find that his father's courage had rubbed off on him, and he continued the reforms that King Asa had started.

What does the author say about Jehoshaphat?

His father Asa modeled for his son what it looked like to stand against the tide and speak truth to restore Judah by turning the people away from idol worship. King Jehoshaphat not only removed the high places that his father neglected to remove but took the Asherim out of Judah. This was the Canaanite fertility goddess, also referred to as the Asherah or Asherah poles, erected for idol worship.

Read 2 Chronicles 15:16–17: *What else did Asa model for his son?*

EXCAVATE

Telling the truth to a family member to change the course of sin in a generation likely didn't come easy. But King Asa followed through on his commitment to God, gathered his courage, and kicked his mom's idols to the curb. We ultimately answer to no man or woman, even if it is a close family member, but only to God. We and we alone are held responsible for our obedience.

This can cause great angst in a family to break the bondage of sin, but I love how Scripture refers to both Asa, the father, and Jehoshaphat, the son, as having the courage to follow God instead of the family rules.

I grew up in a home with an angry father, and he passed that on to his children. He surrendered his anger to God when I was a teenager. He learned to manage it, but it wasn't until I was married and had children that I saw the transformation.[7] It was something I had to come to terms with as a believer, and I knew that I didn't want to pass anger on to my children, as tempting as it was to justify my outbursts as a young mother. The frightened look on my oldest son's face as he backed away from me when he was three years old was enough to convince me that I needed to get my anger under the control of the Holy Spirit.

As I managed my anger, God captured my attention in a unique way when I saw the movie *Tombstone*[8] in the theater. This classic western tells the story of Wyatt Earp and his brothers cleaning up the Wild West from all the bad guys in Tombstone, Arizona. A portion of the movie highlights one of the bad guys, Ringo, who Doc Holliday refers to as having a black heart of hatred, anger, and violence.

Let me back up here. When I was growing up, my dad would tell us stories of a relative on his side of the family who rode with the Ringo Brothers. Later, as I did some genealogical research, I learned that Ringo was my great-grandmother's uncle. The same dude in the movie. When I was in the theater and saw the evil and hatred that this man displayed, I had to excuse myself and leave the theater. I was undone with grief and sadness over the way Ringo's anger had become a thread in our family history. On the way home that night, I asked God to remove the black stain on our heritage and help me break the chain of anger and rage in our family, starting with me.

FIELDNOTES

How about you? How can you stand for truth in order to break the sin in your life or family tree? Talk to God about it and ask Him to give you the courage He gave to Asa and Jehoshaphat.

FRIENDLY ALLIANCES AND COSTLY ALIGNMENT

Looking back over your regnal formula chart for Jehoshaphat you will notice in the synchronism column that Jehoshaphat ascends the throne during the reign of King Ahab of Israel. Ahab became king when Jehoshaphat's father Asa was in the thirty-eighth year of his reign (1 Kings 16:29).

First Kings 16:29–33 lists all the evil and idolatry Ahab commits and then finishes with, "Ahab did more to provoke the LORD, the God of Israel, to anger than all the kings of Israel who were before him." He had a partner in crime in his wife Jezebel, who has been referred to as one of the evilest women in biblical times. Her hatred for Yahweh and her seeking to kill the prophets of God are only some of her evil deeds, let alone her worship of Baal. God sent many warnings to Ahab, all of which he refused to heed. Nearly six and a half chapters of 1 Kings tell of the downfall of Jehoshaphat's counterpart King Ahab.

Yet, in Chronicles, we find that Jehoshaphat has decided to make a marriage alliance between his son Jehoram and Ahab's daughter, Athaliah. (These two will come up in next week's study—stay tuned!) This, as we will find, has a lasting impact, not only on their generation but the generations to follow.

Read the story of Ahab's invitation to Jehoshaphat in 2 Chronicles 18:3–26.

What is the contrast between Ahab's method of inquiring of the Lord compared to that of King Jehoshaphat?

Why was Ahab so upset with the prophet Micaiah?

Describe what happens in 2 Chronicles 18:28–34.

Now, look at 2 Chronicles 19:1–3; what happened, and why was Jehoshaphat rebuked?

What lesson do you think he learned after Ahab's death?

EXCAVATE

I want to close this week with a sobering truth, one that I hope will cause us all to think about how our alliances not only impact us but those closest to us. When King Jehoshaphat died, his son Jehoram ascended the throne. What you are about to read I find very disturbing, but there is a lesson here for everyone.

Read 2 Chronicles 21:1–6.

Briefly describe what happened. Who died?

Even though Jehoram was a king in Judah, what does verse 6 say about him? What king is he likened to?

I can't help but notice who Jehoram married: Ahab's daughter, Athaliah. We can only guess that her influence over Jehoshaphat's son was not positive and did not lead him to follow God as his father had. Just as God rebuked Solomon for allowing his wives to turn his heart against God, evil was also prevalent in the house of Ahab and his wife Jezebel.

It shouldn't surprise us what happened to the rest of Jehoshaphat's family. He had set up his children and his sons to secure the borders around Judah by giving them the fortified cities and the wealth to maintain their rule. Perhaps Jehoram's siblings and some of the princes of Israel were a threat to Jehoram and he felt the need to grab all he could, but 2 Kings 8:18 says he walked in the ways of the house of Ahab. All this we could speculate is because of his father King Jehoshaphat's alliance with King Ahab.

King Jehoshaphat's "25-year reign included some of the highest points of faith in the Lord and lowest points of failure to trust in the Lord."[9] One need only read 2 Chronicles 20 to see his incredible trust in God to deliver him from three strong enemies who had come to destroy Judah. I can't help but wonder if the ending of his friendship with Ahab after his death when this great victory took place freed him from the evil influence. You can read more about the alliance between King Ahab of Israel and King Jehoshaphat in 2 Chronicles 18. In the midst of his reign are also some of the lowest points.

I hope we can see here as we finish this week how the alliances we make, whether in friendship or family, impact our children. Since we spend most of our time with the people we enter into partnership with, it's vital that we share the same values. Otherwise, we run the risk of not only exposing ourselves to temptation but exposing our children. This isn't to say that we don't encourage our children to spend time with others who aren't Christ followers. We also can't choose every family member. We want to be a light and influence others for Jesus.

Ultimately, all our relationships have the potential to impact our relationship with God, for good or for evil.

FIELDNOTES

We started this week by looking at the heart of revival. Revival keeps our hearts soft and close to God and helps keep our alliances in check. This critical first pillar of *Reviving Obedience* helps drive us to faithful living with a lasting influence.

As we close, let's also reflect on our alliances in friendship and family and ask some tough questions. Have I allowed a friendship or close ties with a family member to influence me away from my faith in God? Have I allowed myself to make small compromises due to their influence?

Despite the mistakes that Kings Asa and Jehoshaphat made, they both dared to do the right thing (2 Chron. 15:8; 17:6). The two key markers that were a credit to their reign was that they both removed the high places in Judah, and they directed the people to seek the Lord. We can apply this by removing the high places in our own lives and being obedient to continue doing so and seek the Lord—this will keep our hearts soft toward revival. The riveting effect is that removing our own high places keeps our path of faithfulness secure and our influence abounding in long-lasting goodness.

As you've reflected on the questions above regarding alliances and the influence of others, write out a prayer to God listing the small compromises you might have made. Ask God to help you be aware of what needs to change to keep your heart soft toward continual revival.

PRAYER

Dear God . . .

High Places

In the Old Testament, high places are called *bamah* in Hebrew which means "high place," "height," or "back of an animal."[10] The term *bamah* appears over a hundred times in Scripture in reference to a religious site. The worshipers at these high places burned incense or offered sacrifices. In Israel, *bamah* were sites of worship and located at the summits of hills. They were often open and natural areas, but the term *bamah* also can mean a structure. Most likely they were predominantly of Canaanite origin. The Canaanites had no temples, so they built smaller shrines or altars to worship. As the Israelites settled into the land and established permanent structures, temples replaced high places as the central place of worship.

Early in Israel's history, high places were considered acceptable places of worship (1 Sam. 7:17, Ramah; 1 Sam. 10:5, 13, Gibeah-Elohim; and 1 Kings 3:4, Gibeon). The *Lexham Bible Dictionary* gives an explanation as to why they might have been acceptable before the temple was built.

Samuel the prophet worshiped at a high place (see 1 Sam. 9:11–13). There is no indication in this passage that this was not acceptable or a reflection on his ministry. We can conclude that the use of high places was approved because there was no temple during that time where sacrifices could be offered.[11]

Read 1 Kings 3:2–3. What do these verses say about these early high places of worship?

After Solomon built the temple, it became the only acceptable site of worship, and the high places were condemned as religious sites to offer sacrifices. During the reigns of Ahaz and Manasseh, there were high places in the valley of Ben Hinnom that were used for the unthinkable ritual of child sacrifice. God noted these places as evil and forbade these places be used to worship Him. And yet, as we will discover, worship at the high places abounded, even after the reforming kings Asa, Jehoshaphat, Hezekiah, and Josiah broke down the previous generations of altars. But they were never completely removed. Archaeological expeditions in Syria and Palestine have revealed open-air platforms and altars supposedly associated with cultic sites.[12]

After both the kingdoms of Israel and Judah went into exile, Ezekiel 43:6–9 uses the high places as examples of the worst sort of evil. The prophet refers to the kings as defiling God's holy name by consorting with temple prostitutes and committing detestable acts during their reign. All these passages about the high places in the books of Kings and Chronicles reveal that the people of God confused the Canaanite high places of worship with the earlier acceptable high places of worship before the temple was built.

Why do you think the high places were such an affront to God after the temple was constructed?

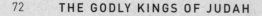

KING JOASH

RENEWING TRUST

Given by the Lord[1]

"And Jehoash did what was right in the eyes of the LORD all his days,
because Jehoiada the priest instructed him."
2 KINGS 12:2

Reality TV has taken over television entertainment, and it seems there isn't any part of life represented that doesn't have a reality show today. As if we don't have enough drama already in our lives. Last year my husband got hooked on a reality show called *Alone*.[2] Ten people are thrust out into the wilderness with ten items of their choosing and a video camera kit. They are isolated from one another, and the goal is to survive in the wilderness the longest. Participants are left alone to endure hunger, cold, and isolation. The prize? $500,000. Sound appealing? No, thank you. However, out of curiosity, I have watched a few episodes with my husband, and after a few episodes, I decided it's not my cup of tea.

We could say that this next king we are about to study comes with his own personal reality TV show that revolves around several members of his family. Are you ready to continue our biblical dig? We are about to launch into some high family

drama this week and to focus on the next pillar of faithful living for lasting influence—*Renewing Trust.* As we explore our next king, we will discover the significance of trust and how it impacts our relationship with God.

One other note as we begin: In the English Standard Version of 2 Kings 11 and 12, this king is referred to as Jehoash. In 2 Chronicles 23 and 24, he is referred to as Joash. For the sake of consistency, we will refer to him as King Joash since many other translations refer to him as Joash.

HIGH DRAMA IN THE KINGDOM

Before God launched me into teaching and writing, I was the creative arts director at our church. You could say I was involved in high drama several months during the year. Each Christmas season we had an event called Christmas Dessert Theatre. The event gave everyone the opportunity to invite friends to enjoy a festive evening and hear a message of hope. We lavished our guests from the moment they arrived with valet parking, extravagant décor, and a scrumptious dessert. As the lights dimmed, familiar Christmas tunes sung in a Broadway-style musical set the stage for the Christmas message.

From performers to servers, this event involved our entire church, and it was a herculean effort to organize the many volunteers. Our strategy was to make visitors feel like honored guests and to introduce them to Jesus. Some of our guests needed their trust renewed, not just in God but in the church and its people. Thousands came through our doors, and each year we witnessed people opening up their hearts to Jesus.

As with any story, there are multiple players who create momentum in the narrative. There are several players in the life of King Joash. On this first day, I want to encourage us to slow down and thoughtfully read. My intent is that we will grasp the overview of Joash's life and the many relationships that played into his ability to trust God.

Read 2 Kings chapters 11–12.

There are forty-two verses between the two chapters. I suggest you grab a cup of coffee or tea, and sit down with your Bible and some highlighters to begin to read the unique way that King Joash ascended the throne. As you read, note the following: key players, significant events, repeated phrases, and observations.

After you are finished reading, write a brief summary of the two chapters as if you were trying to explain Joash's life to someone. You don't have to list all the details, just the most significant.

Who are the primary adults Joash trusts in his early life?

SURVEY

Before we get into the high drama in the story this week, let's complete for King Joash the regnal chart we've filled out for our other three kings.

Reread 2 Kings 12:1–3.

JUDAH REGNAL FORMULA: KING JOASH

	ELEMENTS	KING JOASH OF JUDAH: 2 KINGS 11–12 AND 2 CHRONICLES 22:10–12, 23–24
1	SYNCHRONISM	King Jehu
2	ACCESSION AGE	Seven years old
3	REIGN LENGTH	40 years
4	MOTHER'S NAME	
5	EVALUATION	
6	HIGH PLACES	
7	NARRATIVE MATERIAL	
8	ANNALS REFERENCE	
9	DEATH NOTICE	

There is one family member who isn't listed on the above chart, but who is important because she is a critical player in the story. We will discuss more about her later.

EXCAVATE

Read 2 Chronicles 23–24.

As you did with 2 Kings 11–12, take time to note the key players, significant events, repeated phrases, and observations. We will unpack the details the rest of the week. Today, I want you to soak in the story, reading it several times to see the big picture we will uncover later in the week.

What are the differences, if any, between the account of King Joash in 2 Kings and 2 Chronicles?

FIELDNOTES

I am certain you have found by now that there are multiple details surrounding the reign of King Joash. Let's summarize some of them to better understand his character.

How would you describe Joash's upbringing from this narrative?

What are some things, both negative and positive, that may have shaped his character?

UNTANGLING THE WEB

Now the fun begins. I promise this will be more thrilling than a favorite reality show as we untangle the drama that takes place after King Ahaziah died. His son, the future king, Joash, has some significant women in his early life.

SURVEY

Review the observations you made in Day One after reading chapters in 2 Kings 11–12. Describe these women and Joash's relationship to them:

Athaliah

Jehosheba

Nurse

As we place each of these characters in their respective roles as Athaliah usurps the throne, let's get another look at Joash's grandmother.

Read 2 Kings 8:25–26 and 2 Chronicles 22:3.

Write a brief bio of Athaliah, including her characteristics. You can add any observations you might have from yesterday's reading.

What was her relationship to the royal family?

EXCAVATE

Athaliah's 22-year-old son was dead, and she was angry. So angry that she committed murder, not just once but multiple times, destroying all the royal heirs. Reread 2 Kings 11:1. What do you think her motive was to destroy her family? Was it grief? Power? Both? Athaliah had not only position but power, and she had something else that she didn't even recognize: the ability to influence.

I want to encourage you as we contemplate what we've read so far in Day Two about the women in Joash's life. Please don't minimize your influence as a woman. You have more influence than you realize, and we can choose to either use our influence for godly pursuits or manipulate it for our own purposes. Dear one, the very fact that you are in this study reveals that you have the heart to influence others in a godly way. Let's use our influence for Jesus to impact lives in such a way that we leave a legacy worth following.

FIELDNOTES

Queen Athaliah's commentary is sad, and she grasped power when she could have given truth, love, and wisdom. She broke trust with her loved ones by her murderous deeds and, most tragically, she defied God. Proverbs 14:1 states, "The wisest of women builds her house, but folly with her own hands tears it down." This word "tear" translates as ruin, destroy, pull down.[3]

Athaliah not only tore down her home with her actions, but she also left a stain on Judah. Her evil influence ravaged Judah with six years of continued idol worship before her grandson ascended to the throne.

What does a wise woman do to build her house?

Look up the word "build" in a commentary or concordance to give you greater insight.

Bonds of Trust

This next part of the drama focuses on two godly people who dared to stand against Queen Athaliah. Both of these players had significant roles. Let's look at how they came into the scene that dramatically changed the dynamic of the situation.

SURVEY

Reread 2 Kings 11:4–12.

Who was Jehoiada, and what was his primary responsibility?

Who was he married to? (See 2 Chron. 22:11)

How might you imagine this husband and wife team working together to rescue the prince?

List the characteristics of Jehosheba (also, Jehoshabeath in Chronicles).

EXCAVATE

I can only imagine that Jehoiada and Jehosheba's influence on the young prince was significant as he spent much of his formative years under their care, in their home, and with their children.

What could you surmise Joash would learn living with Jehoiada and Jehosheba?

How important do you think their influence was?

What do you think Joash's trust level would have been with Jehoiada?

FIELDNOTES

We learn from reading this story that there is a strong bond between Joash and his uncle, the priest Jehoiada, and probably with his aunt Jehosheba. She used her resources successfully to rescue the young prince. He was a baby at the time when Athaliah became a madwoman killing the royal heirs of her son, Ahaziah. We can't underestimate the significance of this piece of the story. This couple's influence permeated the rule of Joash, as he became king when he was just seven years old and needed guidance.

Is there someone in your life who needs to be rescued relationally? (I don't mean the enabling, dysfunctional type of saving, but rather God leading you to invest relationally in someone who is in danger of losing their faith.)

Who needs your influence and encouragement?

Take a moment and reflect, asking God to show you if there is anyone in your circle He is calling you to invest in more significantly. Spend some time praying for this person and ask God what next steps He wants you to take.

REFORM AND REPAIRS

One Friday, late in the afternoon, my husband decided that he was the demo dude and proceeded to rip out an old bar with a sink in one of our first homes. Did I mention to you that my husband is a pastor and not a plumber? The one challenge he forgot to factor in was the plumbing. As he tore the cabinets out, he couldn't cap the pipes, so being late in the evening, the only alternative was to turn off the water or have a flood. He assured me he had contacted someone who could come the next day so we wouldn't be without water for more than twelve hours.

There was one small problem. I had a speaking event the following day, and I needed to leave the house early in the morning. Since I'd had no advanced warning about the lack of water, I was a hot mess with dirty hair and was not a happy camper. Repairs were on the way but not soon enough. We look back and laugh at it now, but it was a mess because we had no plan.

As we read Joash's request for repairs to the temple, we will learn that things didn't work out exactly as he planned, and he had to make some adjustments.

SURVEY

Read 2 Kings 12 and 2 Chronicles 24:1–14.

As you have in previous readings, make notes as to key players, repeated phrases, characteristics, and any other observations from these chapters.

Specifically, what did you learn from your reading about King Joash?

What were some of the repairs Joash made to the temple? Why do you suppose the temple was in such disarray?

EXCAVATE

After Joash became an adult, the Bible says that Jehoiada selected two wives for him and Joash had sons and daughters (2 Chron. 24:3). Then Joash decided to repair the temple. After Athaliah's demise, we could assume that since she ruled Judah for six years (2 Kings 11:3) and was influenced by the idolatry of her parents, the temple may have needed repairs. After all, she was the daughter of Ahab, and possibly Jezebel would have been her mother whose evil practices were embedded in her heart.

Because of Athaliah's murderous acts against innocent royal heirs, her children, and even her grandchildren, we might conclude that her actions were born out of revenge and hatred for the house of David. Nothing was going to stop her ambition to rule, not even her offspring.

What would cause a woman to want to kill her children unless she had sold her soul to evil?

Living under Jehoiada's household and his influence, King Joash's desire to repair the temple seems a natural progression to bring about the restoration to worship. He trusted Jehoiada's wisdom, and I am sure his influence led Joash to take these steps.

We've spent a considerable amount of time unraveling the story of King Joash the past few days. We've gained a glimpse of Joash's relationships and how they were built. As we've read, Joash evidently trusted Jehoiada enough for Jehoiada to help him with the temple. There was a strong bond between them. As we uncover more of the story tomorrow, I want you to tuck away this idea of trust.

Look at 2 Kings 12:2 again. What is the reason Joash followed the Lord?

I want to suggest that Joash's relationship with Jehoiada was more significant than his relationship with Jehovah, unlike some of his counterparts who experienced a more direct connection with God. Scripture doesn't give us any more details about his relationship with Jehoiada, but his actions after the death of Jehoiada point to a different reality than the godly actions of his earlier reign.

Think of the people in your life who influence you spiritually; how has their influence affected your willingness to trust God?

How much do you lean on this person(s)? Why?

As we wrap up our time today, talk to God about your ability to trust Him over the voices of others. Ask Him to show you anywhere in your life where you depend on your spiritual influencers more than you rely on and trust Him.

SECONDHAND FAITH

When you watch a reality TV show, there is a climax to the situation featured on the show after several episodes. Producers are skilled at baiting you to keep watching episode after episode because, of course, we want to know what happens!

Likewise, the drama continues for King Joash. Second Chronicles fills in some pretty significant gaps in the story of King Joash that aren't mentioned in 2 Kings 11 and 12. Between 2 Kings 12:16 and 17, there are a whole series of events that take place.

SURVEY

Read 2 Chronicles 24:15–27.

What happens in this account?

Let's go a little deeper by pulling out our scribe skills. In your notebook or journal, write out the verses in 2 Chronicles 24:15–22, then answer the following questions.

What happened to Jehoiada? What does his epitaph say about his faithfulness?

Notice verse 18. What happened here? Describe King Joash's actions. What reasons do you see for the paradigm shift after Jehoiada died?

If we look back to the start of King Joash's reign and what God said about him in the early part of chapter 24, we can see the heart of the matter: "And Joash did what was right in the eyes of the LORD all the days of Jehoiada the priest."

After reading the Chronicles account, would you add anything to your answer to the question we asked earlier about some of the reasons that Joash did what was right as long as Jehoiada the priest was alive?

EXCAVATE

As we think about how living faithfully creates a lasting influence, we need to do so within the framework of our relationship with God. Is it sincere? Is it genuine? Do we trust Him? Or are we riding on the coattails of the peak of faith in others? How can we be certain to renew our trust and keep that pillar strong in our walk with Jesus?

Even when voices of truth confronted Joash, he still did what was wrong, killing his own cousin, Jehoiada's son Zechariah. Maybe at this point, he felt like he was free from the influence of his uncle, and he was going to call the shots. We don't know for sure; the conclusion we might draw is that Joash, rather than leaning on his own faith in God, leaned mostly on Jehoiada's faith as long as Jehoiada was alive.

FIELDNOTES

Growing up in America, going to church, and living in a Christian culture, it's easy to accept the faith of others as your own. How does cultural Christianity sneak in? I believe the temptation to live a secondhand faith comes from depending on others to disciple our hearts. We have to be intentional about the study of God's Word, prayer, and the practice of learning to hear God's voice of truth for ourselves. We have to continually renew our trust in God. Sermons, podcasts, devotionals, and other resources are all great tools to encourage us in the faith, but they're no substitute for sitting down with God's Word and digging out the truth on our own. When we resort to just hearing and reading *about* the Bible, we miss God and learning about who He is and knowing Him better.

We also need to become critical thinkers when it comes to our faith. Part of my role as a university professor is to help my students absorb what they're learning and teach them to wrestle with their learning, which includes reading, studying, discussions, and writing assignments. The same is true for our understanding of God and our relationship with Him. If we only take at face value what we read or hear from others without reflecting on what we hear about God, it doesn't embed itself into our hearts. We become what I like to call marshmallow thinkers, instead of critical thinkers. I can't emphasize this enough.

Sadly, it has been said that biblical literacy is at an all-time low in the history of the church.[4] It is a national church crisis. Is it any wonder we can't discern truth from false teaching and lies?

The writer of Hebrews reminds us of the importance of what a mature believer looks like.

Read Hebrews 5:11–14. *According to this passage, what might having a second-hand faith look like? What do we need to ensure a strong relationship with God?*

As we close this week's study, take a few moments to consider where a secondhand faith may have crept into your heart. Confess it and write it as a prayer below. Make a plan to encourage your faith and relationship in Jesus and renew your trust.

PRAYER

Dear God . . .

The Role of the Priesthood in Judah

To better understand worship in Judah, it's helpful to learn about the significance of the high priest's role and function. The office of the high priest began with Aaron, Moses's brother. In the book of Exodus, chapters 28 and 29, the initial directions are given for everything concerning the role of the priesthood and those who would attend to worship. From the garments they wore to the process of consecrating themselves to carry out their duties, God is very specific on how this role is fulfilled.

The worship in the Old Testament was vastly different than our worship today. After the great exodus of the Israelites from Egypt, God—through Moses—set up strict requirements for how to atone for sin through the blood sacrifices of animals. When Jesus, the promised Messiah, appeared centuries later, His sacrificial death on the cross became what He Himself called the fulfillment of the new covenant (Luke 22:20). His death and resurrection fulfilled the law as it had been practiced in the Old Testament. It was no longer necessary to practice the Old Testament rituals. After Jesus' ascension to heaven, the early church came into existence and a new way of worship was birthed.

The office of the high priest was usually held for life, and in the beginning, the high priests would come from the family of Aaron. The office continued in the line of his son Eleazar for two hundred and ninety-six years with some variation, and then with Zadok of the family of Eleazar (1 Kings 2:35) after Solomon deposed Abiathar and appointed Zadok. This line remained until the captivity of Judah, and after the return from exile back to Israel, the family of Eleazar continued in a succession of further priests.[5]

Among the people, only the priests held and carried out this role, set apart by God. In the time of the kings, the priests were responsible for the day-to-day operations of the temple in Jerusalem and other sites in the surrounding regions of Judah. The high priest might also be referred to as the chief priest, overseeing the other priests as their leader.

One of their primary roles was to oversee the sacrifices and offerings. They were, in fact, ministers of the altar (Joel 1:13). Another significant role of the high priest was his exclusive role to enter the temple's holy of holies and only then on the Day of Atonement. Throughout the reigns of the kings of Judah, the high priest functioned as the primary head of the Jerusalem priesthood. They were often involved politically, as we see in many of the kings' narratives.[6]

You can read further on the specific roles and functions of the priests in relation to the traditions and feasts in Leviticus chapters 16, 21–23.

King Amaziah

RECEIVING WISDOM

Jehovah is Mighty[1]

"And he did what was right in the eyes of the Lord, yet not like
David his father. He did in all things as Joash his father had done."

2 Kings 14:3

Listening well has been a character trait I've had to give some serious attention to.
Being a word person, not to mention a leader and a teacher, I often think the need
to say more takes precedence over the need to listen. Talking more than listening
can get me into a heap of trouble. My friend Becky Harling wrote *How to Listen
So People Will Talk: Build Stronger Communication and Deeper Connection*,[2] a book
that transformed the way I think about listening.

I decided to try out her suggested assessment by asking a few people close to me
about my listening skills. One of the people I chose was my sweet daughter-in-
love, Emily. She's not a huge talker, but she is a great listener, and she knows that I
struggle with entering a room with my mouth first instead of my ears.

When I asked her if she'd be willing to evaluate me, she eagerly accepted the
challenge; but then I didn't hear from her for several weeks. I became nervous and

panicked. "What if it is so bad, she doesn't have the courage to share with me? What if I have been a total failure in our relationship, and she's given up?" The questions whirled around like a tornado. Then one day, she called and said she'd finished the listening survey. We made a date for lunch. I knew I had lots of room to grow, so I was ready to hear what she had to say. So, with trepidation, I practiced my newfound skills and listened intently without interrupting (at least, not too much). She was gracious beyond measure and affirmed me in the process, but pointed out some key areas where I could strengthen my listening, which would help our relationship. She ended by sharing how grateful she was that I still was teachable, and that statement meant more to me than anything.

When we listen, we tune in to how we can improve our relationships and gain wisdom—this includes our relationship with God.

As we study the next godly king, we will see the harsh reality of a heart that chooses when and where to listen; and in the case of King Amaziah, listening to God halfheartedly had severe consequences for Judah. And yet, Amaziah is still in the hall of fame of godly kings. "And he did what was right in the eyes of the LORD, yet not with a whole heart" (2 Chron. 25:2). It's the "not with a whole heart" and his inability to listen, along with his pride, that landed him in trouble.

Are you ready? I am so proud of you and your biblical archeology skills. My prayer for us this week is that we would keep an open heart or, in this case, open ears to hear what God has to say to us through studying the life of King Amaziah. This week, we will look at the third pillar of faithful living for lasting influence— *Receiving Wisdom.*

QUEEN MOM

King Amaziah's mother was named Jehoaddan of Jerusalem. Her name means "Jehovah-pleased."[3] Have you noticed that with several of the kings we are studying, their mother's full name and place of origin are both mentioned? These facts are part of the Regnal Formula and helpful for understanding the history and narrative of each king in the southern kingdom of Judah. It's interesting to note that mothers are only listed in Judah's regnals but not those of the northern kingdom of Israel.

Jehoaddan was a local girl from Jerusalem, so she would have been raised under Jewish customs and laws, unlike many of the other mothers of the kings of Judah. Those mothers were from neighboring provinces and surrounding nations influenced by pagan practices.[4] Given the significance of names in the Jewish culture, she would have most likely been raised to worship Jehovah, following Jewish customs and traditions.

She could also have had extensive knowledge and understanding of Jewish law depending on the spiritual environment of her household. Although Scripture doesn't provide many details about the mothers of the kings, we can speculate that Amaziah was influenced by the faith of his mother (and even her family) and her practice of Jewish law. The queen mothers had significant positions in the royal household and were often, if not always, in charge of the religious training of their sons. This could point to the reason why Amaziah followed Mosaic Law when he killed the servants who murdered his father, but he didn't kill their sons.

And as soon as the royal power was firmly in his hand, he struck down his servants who had struck down the king his father. But he did not put to death the children of the murderers, according to what is written in the Book of the Law of Moses, where the LORD commanded, "Fathers shall not be put to death because of their children, nor shall children be put to death because of their fathers. But each one shall die for his sin." (2 Kings 14:5–6)

Jehoaddan's faithful influence may have also encouraged Amaziah as he chose to listen to the prophet God sent in 2 Chronicles 25:7–8 as he was gathering troops to go up against the Edomites. We will dig into that later, but for now, as we have for the other kings, let's fill in the Judah Regnal Formula to more fully understand the background of Amaziah.

SURVEY

Reread 2 Kings 14:1–4 and read 2 Chronicles 25:1–2.

JUDAH REGNAL FORMULA: KING AMAZIAH

ELEMENTS	KING AMAZIAH OF JUDAH: 2 KINGS 14:1–20 AND 2 CHRONICLES 25
SYNCHRONISM	King Joash of Israel
ACCESSION AGE	
REIGN LENGTH	29 years
MOTHER'S NAME	Jehoaddan (also, Jehoaddin) of Jerusalem
EVALUATION	
HIGH PLACES	
NARRATIVE MATERIAL	
ANNALS REFERENCE	
DEATH NOTICE	

EXCAVATE

Read 2 Kings 14:1–20 and 2 Chronicles 25.

Make any notes of key players, observations, and characteristics.

Write out 2 Chronicles 25:7–11 in your notebook or journal.

What did God say to King Amaziah through the man of God?

What problem did the man of God help King Amaziah solve?

The truth is, our influence is powerful as we peek around the corner and imagine Amaziah's mother and how her influence seeped into her son's reign for him to learn, gain wisdom, and listen. Although Amaziah followed the law and listened to the encounter with the man of God (2 Chron. 25:7–11), he did so halfheartedly for the rest of his reign. We could assume his mother had died, and therefore, her voice of wisdom was removed from his life.

FIELDNOTES

Take a minute and complete a list of your primary roles in your current season and the names of those you influence through those roles. Next to their name, write out one word that describes your direct influence in their life. (Tomorrow we will look at this in more detail.)

A WOMAN'S INFLUENCE

In our little town of Blaine by the sea, we have a statue named the *Vigil* that stands in the square nestled up against the water. The statue depicts four figures, a grandmother, a mother, and her young son holding a dog.[5] The plaque in front reads, "For every fisherman who went to sea, there was a vigil kept by the women who stayed behind waiting for his return. These women provided civilizing influences. They kept the home fires burning, and perpetuated the culture. They taught the young, nursed the sick, and cared for the elderly. They were the steady hands behind the schools, the churches, and the community." The statue is a symbol and tribute to women in Blaine at the turn of the twentieth century. When I walk by the square, it reminds me of how much influence we women have in all aspects of life.

As a mom and grandmother, my prayer is always to leave a godly influence marked by a faithful life devoted to Jesus. It isn't always easy, and I've made plenty of mistakes. My prayer is that my children and grandchildren will witness my obedience and see the faithfulness of God in my life as they've watched me, first up close as a young mom and now as an outside influence sharing my faith with their children. I hope they know my heart's desire above all else is to love Jesus, learn and hear God's voice, and follow in obedience.

I wonder if King Amaziah's mother Jehoaddan felt the same way. A husband and father who was both ruler and king would have had limited contact with his children, and much of the child's influence was shaped by his mother. I wonder, did Jehoaddan make sure her son knew the law by taking him to the temple to learn from the priests? Did she tell him bedtime stories of God delivering the Israelites from Egypt and His wonders in the wilderness? Did she recount the miracle stories about Abraham, Joshua, and Moses? Did she sing him songs of Jehovah and tell him that He and He alone is the one true God? We can only speculate, but Amaziah's actions reveal in part that he did learn about Jewish law and customs and what it looked like to worship God. Although Amaziah made his own decisions, he would most likely know the truth as taught by his mother.

SURVEY

Read 1 Samuel 25.

I want to divert a bit and camp out on this idea of the power of your influence as a woman. We'll look at another story about a king in Scripture and a woman who had a significant impact in a difficult situation. She turned the heart of the future King David from a path of destruction. Her name is Abigail.

As you read, make notes on the main characters in the narrative, noting their characteristics:

Abigail

Nabal

Nabal's Servant

What does the Bible call Nabal? Abigail? What is the contrast?

What did Abigail decide to do? Why?

How did David respond?

How did Abigail's discerning act change David's mind?

What do you think was her strategy? Why?

When I read this story, it reminds me that we have little control over the behavior of others, but we do have control over our responses and actions. We have the power of godly influence to wield as a weapon of strength in difficult circumstances. We learn about Abigail's character when we read what Scripture says about Abigail and Nabal: "Now the name of the man was Nabal, and the name of his wife Abigail. The woman was discerning and beautiful, but the man was harsh and badly behaved; he was a Calebite" (1 Sam. 25:3).

We can conclude that Abigail lived in a tumultuous environment, and most likely this wasn't the first time she had saved her household from the foolish ways of her husband. As Scripture refers to her as beautiful and intelligent, she probably was a sight to behold for David, who was on the march to avenge himself against the insults he'd received from Nabal. She stopped David in his tracks, not because of her outer beauty but because of her wise actions and humble spirit.

Reread verses 24–31 in 1 Samuel 25. *How does Abigail plead her case?*

In verse 24, why do you think she says, "On me alone . . . be the guilt"?

Where does she place her emphasis in her appeal? List what she says about God and what she says about David.

What does verse 28 reveal about Abigail's wisdom?

One of the reasons I felt like God led me to look at this account of Abigail's life is that living a faithful life with lasting influence isn't reminiscent of a neat and tidy life. It is difficult, but it is in our grasp to do so with God's help.

Do you feel stuck in circumstances beyond your control? Are you tired of fighting the battle? As with Abigail, God can make a way for you and for me to navigate a path that is the opposite of strife—even if the situation feels hopeless. In the same way Abigail stated to David, "Because my lord is fighting the battles of the Lord" (1 Sam. 25:28), we also need to believe that God is fighting our battles. God sees the bigger picture, and at that moment when things seem hopeless, we have a choice to lean in and let God strengthen and help. When we are weary, it is tempting to give in and give up. If we throw in the towel and walk away from God and refuse to listen, we run the risk of losing a faithful influence on those around us.

Though King Amaziah's mother influenced her son, she did not have control over his actions. I have to believe that because of her influence, history was changed because, for whatever reason, her son decided to do the right thing early in his reign. He paid attention to the warning from the man of God who exhorted him not to let the army of Israel go with him to fight the Edomites. We will explore in more depth tomorrow.

FIELDNOTES

Think about your current circumstance. Where do you have the power to influence? What might God be saying to you? How can you be an Abigail in your situation? What truth do you need to preach to yourself?

Fill out the chart below. When you are done, ask God to help you continue to preach the truth to yourself in whatever challenge you are facing.

CONCERN/NEED	LIE THAT KEEPS ME FROM BELIEVING GOD	TRUTH TO PREACH

HEART TO LISTEN AND OBEY

When we first start to read about Amaziah, we can celebrate that we are reading about a king who exercised wisdom and listened to God—until he didn't. Then we heave a big sigh and wonder why he went from one extreme to the next. This is what we will try to discover the rest of this week as we use our biblical archeology tools with the Holy Spirit to bring understanding and application to our lives.

Let's practice being a scribe once again by writing 2 Kings 14:1–15 by hand in your notebook or journal.

Look back over what you wrote, and with a highlighter circle everything you find that lines up with "doing what was right in the eyes of the LORD." Now take a second highlighter and circle the events that reflect the opposite.

What did you discover?

SURVEY

Read 2 Chronicles 25:5–11.

We're looking at the book of Chronicles because the author of Kings leaves out some details that might explain some of King Amaziah's actions.

Between verses 6 and 7 in 2 Kings 14, there is a gap of events that reveals Amaziah's obedience and willingness to listen. Chapter 25 in 2 Chronicles fills in this gap and helps us understand Amaziah's obedience in listening to God at the beginning of his reign.

What does 2 Chronicles 25:2 say about this discrepancy in Amaziah's behavior?

Note verses 7–8. Why was the prophet discouraging Amaziah from adding 100,000 mighty men?

What were Amaziah's concerns?

How does the man of God respond?

Write out verse 9 below.

How does God honor Amaziah's obedience to listen to the man of God?

What does verse 11 say about Amaziah's heart?

Have you ever made a plan and been ready to launch, and then God said "don't do this?" What happened?

This story reveals that when God stops us in the middle of our plans, we'd better listen. What are the two phrases the man of God reminded Amaziah of that we should also remember?

1.

2.

EXCAVATE

Faithful living requires us to learn to be good listeners and follow up with obedience when God speaks. Listening precedes receiving wisdom from God. We may not have a specific "man of God" to visit us, but we do have God's Word and wise counselors, which can give us the courage to do the right thing at the right time.

As the man of God told Amaziah, "The LORD is able to give you much more than this" (2 Chron. 25:9), meaning, His ways are higher than our ways (Isa. 55:8–9), and He sees the bigger picture when we only see what is right in front of us.

Not too long ago, I was faced with a listening crisis. I woke up at 3:12 a.m. feeling as though my brain had run a marathon. When I can't sleep, I ask God if He wants me to pray. I often don't wait long enough for Him to answer, and I drift back to sleep. This night was different. Days before, I had found myself in terrible angst, overrun by a crowded schedule.

Most, if not all of us, adapted to a new normal during the global pandemic. During that time, moving from traveling nearly full time to working from home seemed to me like a reprieve. Except for one caveat—I felt I could take on more because I was at home. The temptation to say yes to more ministry led to working 10 to 12 hours a day, and it was sucking the life out of me, depleting my creativity and joy.

On my knees in that early hour, I felt God's presence overwhelm the room and sensed Him leading me to step away from a job I loved. At first, I was in total shock and spent the following weeks praying, fasting, and seeking wise counsel. God's whisper turned to a consistent message with a loving warning. I had stepped out of my lane. Moving out of God's calling had done a fair amount of off-roading away from my focus of writing, teaching, and discipling women to more activity that was good but not focused.

I took the plunge. I obeyed, and I quit my job. At first, I was like a newborn foal with shaky legs, not knowing how to stand, let alone walk. After a few weeks, it was as though a window opened with the fresh air rushing in; I could breathe, and there wasn't the frenetic pace and edge to my spirit.[6]

What I couldn't have foreseen was this: a few months after I listened to God's voice and made the decision to obey, my dad became ill. He never really recovered, which thrust me into a nearly full-time temporary role of coordinating his care, selling his home, moving him to my sister's, and helping him get settled. God knew that I would need that extra time to become the coordinating caregiver for my father. If I had still been on the chaotic train of overextending myself, I never would have been able to love my dad in the way that he has needed me the past several months. And even though I was concerned about God's provision, I learned through my obedience, "The Lord is able to give you much more than this." And guess what? He did precisely that. He gave me exactly what I needed!

FIELDNOTES

Do you have a current situation that God is speaking to you about, yet you hesitate to respond in obedience? What has He been saying?

Read Psalm 37:3–7, and then write the verses in your own words as a prayer that applies to you currently.

PRAYER

Dear God . . .

THE CONSEQUENCES OF NOT LISTENING

We left off yesterday with the positive: Amaziah taking courage and leading his warriors to victory against the Edomites because he chose to listen to God. Now we find a gap. In 2 Kings 14:7–8, the downward spiral we see in 2 Chronicles 25:14–16 becomes clear. And yet, because Amaziah listened and paid attention—and God was gracious—he ended up in the godly kings category, although sadly not with his whole heart.

SURVEY

Read 2 Chronicles 25:14–16.

Reading these verses truly baffles me! How could Amaziah's heart so quickly turn from God when God had given him a victory?

What did the prophet say to Amaziah about his refusal to listen?

What are his consequences?

Before we judge Amaziah too quickly, we have to remember that God decided to list him as one of the kings who "did what was right in the eyes of the Lord" (2 Kings 14:3). However, even in this story of Amaziah and his downfall, there is a crucial lesson for us to embrace. People can change in the twinkling of an eye. We can go from a victory to a downward spiral if we don't protect the core of our spirituality. That core is our heart for God.

King Asa is an excellent example of this. After trusting a foreign ruler instead of leaning on God for a solution, Asa received an important reminder in 2 Chronicles 16:9: "For the eyes of the Lord run to and fro throughout the earth, to give strong support to those whose heart is blameless toward him." Another translation puts it this way with a punch at the end of the verse: "The eyes of the Lord search the whole earth in order to strengthen those whose hearts are fully committed to him. What a fool you have been! From now on you will be at war" (NLT).

Here is the truth I am desperate for you to grasp: it all comes down to our hearts.

Read the following Scriptures about the heart and write your observations.

Jeremiah 17: 9

Proverbs 4:23

Hebrews 3:12

Matthew 6:21

Fill in the words from the verses listed, which instruct us how to have a heart for God.

1. Create in me a _____ heart, O God, and _____ a _____ spirit within me. (Ps. 51:10)

2. _____ me wisdom in the _____ heart. (Ps. 51:6)

3. [We] ought always to _____ and not _____ heart. (Luke 18:1)

4. _____ the LORD your God with all your_____ and with all your_____ and with all your _____. (Matt. 22:37)

After reviewing the above verses, what do you think Amaziah missed?

EXCAVATE

Let's be honest; you and I miss the mark as well from time to time. We are human. We make mistakes, and yet God is merciful when we make mistakes and then repent; but what makes Him angry is when we blatantly turn Him off and stop listening, refusing to repent and acting in our own strength. Amaziah's heart was revealed in his response when God held him to account.

Read 2 Chronicles 25:16. How did Amaziah react to the prophet? What does this reveal about his character and his heart to follow God?

His first response was to be defensive rather than listen and take in the prophet's message. King Amaziah cut him off in mid-sentence, threatened him, and didn't let him finish speaking because Amaziah was bent on doing it his way. He went from not listening to God's warning to making a new plan to come against Israel. This was the beginning of Amaziah's demise and reveals his inability to receive wisdom.

Our ability to leave a godly legacy of faithful living depends on whether we are willing to listen and obey God, whether we feel like it or not. We live in a culture in which truth is watered down and based on our feelings. Today's truth is tomorrow's lies, and today's lies are tomorrow's truth. Everything is so muddled, and now more than ever before, we must stand on the truth of God's Word! I can't say it strongly enough.

The future generation of Christ followers depends on our being fully committed with a whole heart and not picking and choosing when we will listen to God. There is a pattern in the narratives of the kings—the ones who listened prospered and were blessed by God. The ones who refused ended their reigns in disaster. We can change the history of our family with godly and faithful living. May it be so that we would live with a humble heart, ever seeking God with everything we have and everything we are because of Him.

As we end our lesson today, set aside a few minutes to search your heart, and ask God to reveal any place you have shut Him out. Ask yourself, Have I cut God off in mid-sentence, tuning Him out to do my own thing?

Ask God as David prayed, "Create in me a clean heart, O God, and renew a right spirit within me" (Ps. 51:10). Pray Psalm 51:1–12 to end your time and sit in His presence humbly, receiving grace and forgiveness to renew your heart and give you a heart to receive wisdom.

Final Defeat

I wish I could say that Amaziah rallied after his last encounter with the prophet God sent to warn him. But sadly, the prophet's words came true: "I know that God has determined to destroy you, because you have done this and have not listened to my counsel" (2 Chron. 25:16). Amaziah didn't waver in closing off his lifeline to Jehovah God. He not only turned his face from God but stopped listening altogether. His sin led him to his final legacy, which was ruin and humiliation.

We all have a choice. In my mid-twenties, I heard one of my mentors share with a group of women that many of our choices over the next ten years would determine the pattern of our influence for the following decades of life. I have never forgotten her words; they have been burned into my memory when I feel stuck and in crisis. I remember that the decisions I choose to make will have a lasting impact, not just for me but also for those around me.

SURVEY

Read 2 Chronicles 25:17–28 and 2 Kings 14:8–14.

Note the similarities in the two accounts. What extra information do we learn about God?

How does this explain the events that followed Amaziah's refusal to listen to the prophet?

Look up Galatians 6:6–10. What does this passage tell us about the law of sowing and reaping?

Describe what you think it means to mock God.

Why is this a severe offense in God's eyes?

What happened to Amaziah, Jerusalem, and the temple when Amaziah didn't listen to the prophet God sent to him? See 2 Chronicles 25:20–24.

Make a list of the sequence of events.

What steps can we take to ensure we don't fall into the same trap as Amaziah in our response to the truth?

EXCAVATE

One of the most common mistakes we make when others are speaking is formulating our response instead of actively listening, pausing, and reflecting. Had Amaziah been truly present, paused, and reflected on the words of the prophets, the destruction for himself and Jerusalem could have been avoided. Instead, he was carried off by his rival Israel, Jerusalem was partially destroyed, and the treasures were stolen. All because he didn't listen, but more so, because of idolatry.

Read 2 Chronicles 25:20. *What does this verse say about God's part in the event?*

Paul speaks in Colossians about the specifics of idolatry. What is the list that he gives in Colossians 3:5?

What else might you add to the list?

Read 1 Samuel 13:14 and Acts 13:22. *What does God say about David in these verses?*

When thinking about the kings of Israel and Judah, I often wonder why King David is evaluated this way. David was by no means perfect. He committed adultery, was a murderer, lied to a priest, disobeyed God, and had many other shortcomings. But there is one thing God said about David in 1 Kings 11:4: "When Solomon was old his wives turned away his heart after other gods, and his heart was not wholly true to the LORD his God, as was the heart of David his father."

The chapter recounts all the sins of idolatry that Solomon practiced and how it angered God. This is something his father David never stooped to, creating and worshiping other gods. He may have been many things, but David was not an idolater. He was a God chaser and sought God continually, he repented when he sinned, and God was merciful to forgive. He lived to the end of his days to make the name of God famous throughout the ancient Near East. His writing still impacts us today in the Psalms, as we have been comforted and also encouraged to exalt God above all else.

Are you getting the picture? God doesn't expect us to be perfect to be faithful. We can choose as David did to be a God chaser, one who stops and listens and doesn't run ahead of God. When we shut God out and refuse to listen, we are at the precipice of inviting idolatry into our life and choosing self-sufficiency and independence apart from God.

We may not see our self-sufficiency that way because we think of idolatry as other things, but our independence apart from God qualifies as idolatry. When, like Amaziah, we turn our face from God and decide to do it our way, He will turn the tide of events and leave us to our own consequences. He does that because He loves us so much and waits for us to cry out to Him for help. He is a patient, loving God waiting for you and for me to choose Him in our weakness.

This is serious stuff, and I hope you can see from studying the life of Amaziah how much God wants us to choose Him. He longs for us to hear His voice and to listen. He longs for us to receive His wisdom. I am learning this firsthand because my word for the year is SLOW. What does this mean? In a nutshell, I believe God wants to teach me to be more present. There has been more chaos than I'd like to admit the past several months, and God keeps reminding me in my angst not to make choices quickly, to slow down long enough to sit, be still, and listen to His voice. He will make things clear if I slow down. That is what I have been focusing on, and I tell you, it has been complicated! I've messed up more times than I want to admit, but I think I am getting the hang of it after half the year has passed.

As we close out this week, look back over your answers, particularly in Day Four: The Consequences of Not Listening. As you review, reflect on your influence and power as a woman to change the space you live in if you are feeling challenged.

Sit with God for a few moments and ask Him to reveal to you what is your next godly step. Write it out as a prayer in the prayer section. If you don't hear anything right away, it's okay. Be patient. God will find you and give you the next step. Anticipate, be present, and listen for His still, small voice. And to help you, stop and pray Psalm 46:10 as David encouraged us to "Be still, and know that I am God."

PRAYER

Dear God . . .

Queen Mothers and Their Influence

It wasn't uncommon for a king to have several wives and concubines. What sets these mothers apart in their respective households from the royal harem is they each bore the son who became heir to the throne. Because of that, they held an important position in the royal household. The term often used in the Hebrew Bible for these women is the term *gebira*, which means a "woman with great authority and power, or queen or queen mother."[7] In many cases, they had control and power second only to the king and had tremendous influence. We see this in 2 Chronicles 22:3 with King Ahaziah, as Scripture testifies that his mother, Queen Athaliah, was his counselor: "He also walked in the ways of the house of Ahab, for his mother was his counselor in doing wickedly." As we learned, Queen Athaliah had one agenda, and her hunger for power caused her to usurp Judah's throne by killing the rest of the royal household except for Joash, who was rescued by his aunt Jehosheba (also, Jehoshabeath).

I thought it might be fun to draw some more profound conclusions about the kings and the influence of their mothers. I've listed all the kings of Judah, including the evil ones. The kings we are studying are in bold.

Look up the corresponding verses, and beside the mother's name, list any other details you find (i.e., the daughter of, etc.) Note under each name from your research any connections of their influence on their sons. Add any other observations you find.

KING	SCRIPTURE	MOTHER
REHOBOAM	1 KINGS 14:21	Naamah the Ammonite
ABIJAM	1 KINGS 15:3	Maacah
ASA	1 KINGS 15:10	Maacah (grandmother)
JEHOSHAPHAT	1 KINGS 22:42	Azubah, the daughter of Shilhi
JEHORAM	2 KINGS 8:16	no mother listed
AHAZIAH	2 KINGS 8:26	Athaliah, the granddaughter of Omri of Israel
JOASH	2 KINGS 12:1	Zibiah of Beersheba
AMAZIAH	2 KINGS 14:2	Jehoaddan of Jerusalem (also, Jehoaddin)
AZARIAH (UZZIAH)	2 KINGS 15:2	Jecoliah of Jerusalem
JOTHAM	2 KINGS 15:33	Jerusha (also, Jerushah), the daughter of Zadok
AHAZ	2 KINGS 16:2	no mother listed

KING	SCRIPTURE	MOTHER
HEZEKIAH	2 KINGS 18:2	Abi, the daughter of Zechariah
MANASSEH	2 KINGS 21:1	Hephzibah
AMON	2 KINGS 21:19	Meshullemeth, the daughter of Haruz of Jotbah
JOSIAH	2 KINGS 22:1	Jedidah, the daughter of Adaiah of Bozkath
JEHOAHAZ	2 KINGS 23:31	Hamutal, the daughter of Jeremiah of Libnah
JEHOIAKIM	2 KINGS 23:36	Zebidah, the daughter of Pedaiah of Rumah
JEHOIACHIN	2 KINGS 24:8	Nehushta, the daughter of Elnathan of Jerusalem
ZEDEKIAH	2 KINGS 24:18	Hamutal, the daughter of Jeremiah of Libnah

As you look over your observations, what conclusions can you draw from the godly kings when compared to the evil kings? What do we learn about listening to God in obedience?

King Uzziah and King Jotham

RELENTLESS FAITH

Uzziah — My strength is Jehovah[1]

"He did what was right in the eyes of the LORD,
according to all that his father Amaziah had done."
2 KINGS 15:3

Jotham — Jehovah is Perfect[2]

"He did what was right in the eyes of the LORD,
according to all that his father Uzziah had done."
2 KINGS 15:34

Do you ever feel like your back is up against a wall, and no matter how hard you try, the battle seems fiercer than ever? Well then, my friend, you are in a good place. Space where God can work and move in ways that you haven't seen Him move before. Space where He can show Himself omnipotent and, at times, even do the impossible in your circumstance. Trust me, it's all worth it—every tear you've cried in your dark place and every prayer you've whispered in the middle of the night. God hears, He knows, and He hasn't forgotten you. His truth will

rescue your tired and weary spirit. This week, we will look at the fourth pillar of faithful living for lasting influence—***Relentless Faith.***

My maternal grandmother had relentless faith, and there isn't a day that goes by I don't think about her. She lived through incredible hardship when she was a young girl in Ukraine until she came to America as a married woman with her family in 1950. As a teenager, her faith carried her through marauding soldiers terrorizing her village, and she lived through starvation and the horrors of WWII.

She gave birth in a refugee camp in Germany, then crossed the Atlantic Ocean to America. Leaving her teenage son behind broke her heart. He had been taken by Russian soldiers and sent to Siberia to a work camp. He was released a few years later and created a new life for himself in another part of the country. My grandparents were separated from their son and his family for the rest of their lives, with the exception of one six-week visit to the United States. The stories she and my grandfather told were threaded with the faithfulness and the miracles of a sovereign God. When I feel like giving up, their godly legacy encourages me to push through and lean in a bit tighter. I believe that if God was faithful to my grandparents, He will be faithful to me in my circumstances. Honestly, my hardships feel minuscule compared to the suffering my grandmother endured. But I also know it is her legacy of faith and prayers that renew my hope in the promises found in God's Word.

This week we will fortify ourselves and learn how to have relentless faith by studying King Uzziah and King Jotham, who are father and son, respectively. I am hoping by the end of this week, you will adopt a godly strategy to know how to be relentless in the battle and be encouraged even if your feet are tired and your arms are heavy.

THE KING WITH TWO NAMES

Azariah, as he is named in the books of Kings, or Uzziah, as he is named in the books of Chronicles, is one in the same person. There is only one letter off in Hebrew, which changes the meaning of his name slightly. Azariah means "helped by Jehovah," and Uzziah means "strength of Jehovah."[3] Azariah, the king mentioned here, is not to be confused with Azariah the priest who is also mentioned in our reading today. (I did warn you in Week One that the books of Kings can be confusing with the various names!)

The books of Kings give only seven verses describing his reign of fifty-two years, while Chronicles dedicates a whole chapter to depicting his life. This study will refer to him as Uzziah since we will mainly study his account in Chronicles. There are a few interesting facts to note as we start using our biblical archeology tools of surveying and excavating. Let's see how sharp your observation skills are.

Read 2 Chronicles 26:1–5.

What do you notice, if anything, that is different about the way the author introduces Uzziah from the other kings we have studied so far?

Now, look again at verse 5. What is the qualifier for Uzziah's success?

"As long as he sought the LORD, God made him prosper." Hold on to this phrase as we keep digging for truth.

SURVEY

Reread 2 Kings 15:1–7 and read 2 Chronicles 26:1–5

Now fill in the Regnal Formula for Uzziah.

JUDAH REGNAL FORMULA: KING UZZIAH

ELEMENTS	KING AZARIAH/UZZIAH OF JUDAH: 2 KINGS 15:1–7 AND 2 CHRONICLES 26
SYNCHRONISM	King Jeroboam of Israel
ACCESSION AGE	
REIGN LENGTH	
MOTHER'S NAME	Jecoliah of Jerusalem
EVALUATION	
HIGH PLACES	
NARRATIVE MATERIAL	
ANNALS REFERENCE	
DEATH NOTICE	

Read 2 Chronicles 26. *Note any observations about this second account of Uzziah, paying close attention to key players, characteristics, and repeated phrases.*

From your notes, what are some of the primary characteristics of King Uzziah?

In your overview, what have you noticed about Uzziah that is different from his father King Amaziah?

EXCAVATE

A bit of chocolate cake and a great historical series on Netflix provide a needed break. But when I want to give up, the temptation is to spend days and days eating cake and watching Netflix. Then God gently reminds me that a warrior doesn't train on the leather sectional with a cozy animal print blanket, chocolate mousse, and Masterpiece Theater.

A warrior trains by being prepared and suiting up with armor from God's Word. That is what we will do this week as we strengthen ourselves in the Lord Jesus Christ, so we can have unwavering faith and stand firm!

What is your temptation when your heart wants to give up?

FIELDNOTES

Today we are collecting background on our king before we move into the details of his reign.

As you've read both accounts of Uzziah in Kings and Chronicles, what are your main observations about Uzziah in comparison to the other kings we've studied up to this point?

Tuck these observations away as we begin using our tools to explore and uncover more treasures in God's Word.

THREE STRATEGIES FOR STAYING IN THE BATTLE

Fortifying our faith is an essential piece of faithful living and lasting influence. We can't just stumble into the battle. We have to prepare and launch a strategy to defeat our enemy, the devil, both inside and out. Relentless faith is built on having a battle plan. This week I suggest three ways we can fortify ourselves by looking at the life of Uzziah. We will do a brief overview and then look at the three strategies in depth over the next two days of our study.

SURVEY

Here is an overview of three strategies for staying in the battle. To start, you need to:

1. Surround yourself with the right voices.

Read 2 Chronicles 26:5. *Whose is the voice that Uzziah listens to?*

2. Know your enemy.

Read 2 Chronicles 26:6–8. *List Uzziah's enemies and whom he conquered.*

3. Prepare your armor.

Read 2 Chronicles 26:14–15. *List the pieces of armor that Uzziah provided his entire army.*

Before we dive into the three strategies in depth I want to give you some background on Uzziah. King Uzziah reigned successfully and for a long time—fifty-two years. Part of his strategy was to reclaim what had been lost in the previous generations. He strategized and immediately went out and rebuilt Eloth and restored it to Judah (2 Chron. 26:2). Eloth was a seaport at the Gulf of Aqaba that belonged to the Edomites. The people of Israel passed by Eloth during their wilderness journey, and King Solomon used the port for ship-making.[4]

If you recall, Uzziah's father Amaziah conquered Edom, so Eloth was an important seaport.

Uzziah then proceeded to make war against the Philistines. Read the following verses and circle all the verbs of action that Uzziah accomplished:

> He went out and made war against the Philistines and broke through the wall of Gath and the wall of Jabneh and the wall of Ashdod, and he built cities in the territory of Ashdod and elsewhere among the Philistines. God helped him against the Philistines and against the Arabians who lived in

Gurbaal and against the Meunites. The Ammonites paid tribute to Uzziah, and his fame spread even to the border of Egypt, for he became very strong. (2 Chronicles 26:6–8)

Name the enemies he conquered. (You'll read about these nations in the Artifacts: Digging Deeper section.)

EXCAVATE

I promise you that all this history we are learning is going to come full circle. Let's start with the first strategy: surround yourself with the right voices. All the kings (including Uzziah) who were successful during their reign listened to the voices that came through messengers, such as prophets, seers, or "the man of God."

Read 2 Chronicles 26:5, and write out the verse.

What does the Bible say about the voice of Zechariah?

This Zechariah is not to be confused with the prophet Zechariah in the book of the Bible named for him. The identity of the Zechariah in Chronicles is unknown, but this prophet was a mentor and a voice for Uzziah.[5]

Read the following verses in Proverbs and fill in the chart. What do these verses say about listening to the right voice and the consequences if you don't?

VERSE	BENEFITS OF LISTENING TO TRUTH	CONSEQUENCE OF NOT LISTENING
PROVERBS 1:7		
PROVERBS 11:14		
PROVERBS 12:15		
PROVERBS 15:22		
PROVERBS 19:20–21		

FIELDNOTES

Think about the voices you listen to the most often in your life, and write them in the space below.

Which of these people encourage you toward God? Which do you have a hard time convincing that God can be trusted in your circumstances?

As you look through your list, reflect on how much you allow each of these people entry into your heart. Is there anyone who needs to take more of a back seat? Anyone who might need to take more of a role in your life?

You did awesome today! This is such significant digging we are doing, and tomorrow we will look at the second strategy, know your enemy, and the last strategy of what it looks like to prepare your armor.

RELENTLESS ARMOR

Yesterday we explored the first strategy of surrounding yourself with the right voices. As I am writing this study and reviewing the voices in my own life, one person, in particular, has been a consistent voice for decades. Linnea is the mom of one of my childhood friends. As a high schooler, I probably spent more time at Linnea and Gene's house than at my own home. She was not only the mom of my best friend, Sharla, but she is a strong woman of faith.

Linnea modeled for me what it looks like to be a godly woman, more by her actions than by her words. She loves the Word of God, and it slipped from her tongue, not as religious talk but rather as her very life and breath. She is a woman of prayer, and in the past few years, we've been able to spend a little more time together. She is consistent in leaving me with a holy word of encouragement and a loving reminder that she is praying for anything I might share. I count Linnea's voice as a messenger of wisdom and truth; she doesn't sugarcoat anything, and for that, I admire and respect her deeply. Voices of truth are necessary if we are going to stay relentless in the battle of faith.

The second strategy for preparing for battle and building relentless faith is to know your enemy. We'll look at that next.

Uzziah, after he became King, assessed his enemies and made a plan of attack. Just as Uzziah sought to "wage war" against them, we ought to be wise and know who our enemy is and be aware of his schemes.

Before we dig in with our biblical archaeological tools, assess where you currently stand with your enemy, the devil. Circle the number that most closely applies.

1	2	3	4	5	6	7
Satan doesn't exist.	I am not sure if he exists.		He exists, but I don't need to worry about him.			I believe he is real, and I want to be equipped to fight the battle.

Peter says this about Satan in 1 Peter 5:8: "Be sober-minded; be watchful. Your adversary the devil prowls around like a roaring lion, seeking someone to devour." Other translations use the words "walks about" (NKJV), "sneaking around" (CEV). Notice the writer says he "prowls" around like a lion. Sometimes, we believe he is more powerful than he is. We think he is the lion coming after us, and yes, he sneaks around prowling and stalking believers, but it says *like* a lion, not that he *is* a lion.

There is only one who is more powerful and is compared to a lion, but He is referred to as the Lion of Judah in Revelation. "Behold, the Lion of the tribe of Judah, the Root of David, has conquered, so that he can open the scroll and its seven seals" (Rev. 5:5). In these verses, Jesus is the lion and the conqueror, but He is also the lamb slaughtered as a sacrifice for us. He is the almighty powerful Lion of Judah who conquered Satan, and He is our ally to help us in the battle.

Read the preceding verses, 1 Peter 5:6–7. *What do the verses indicate is a prerequisite for knowing the enemy's tactics?*

Next, read verses 9 and 10. *Why do you think the author refers to our enemy in the context of suffering?*

We are more vulnerable when we are struggling. The enemy knows this and purposefully tries to poke at our weak spots in the hopes we will give up on God and lose faith. He probes and prods, and it can seem like he is winning the battle. But don't be confused; as Mark Bubeck says in his book *Warfare Praying*, "There is urgent necessity to know that Satan is not invincible. He is always 'second best.' He is a mere creature, no match for the Creator!"[6]

Read the promise in the last half of 1 Peter 5:10. *What does Peter say will happen after a little while?*

This is God's promise to you and me; He "will himself restore, confirm, strengthen, and establish you." Did you catch the beauty of the two little words "will himself"? God will take care of it; He will see to it that you are restored, confirmed, strengthened, and on top of all that, He will "establish you." That should make our hearts sing with ecstatic joy! God is the restorer of all things and because of this, we can trust Him when we are suffering.

It's critical that we know and understand our enemy and know how he operates, so we aren't caught off guard.

What do the following verses say about Satan's tactics? Is there a theme?

John 8:44

2 Corinthians 4:4

2 Corinthians 11:13–15

2 Corinthians 11:3

Revelation 12:10

How does learning the tactics about our enemy help you in your current circumstance?

What lie has Satan twisted into "truth" in your life?

Here is the good news: God doesn't send us out on the battlefield alone, and He does not leave us to fight alone. He gives us precise instructions to be alert and prepared to withstand the flaming arrows Satan will throw at us. Just as Uzziah prepared his troops, we are to put on the whole armor of God the apostle Paul describes in the book of Ephesians. A soldier going out to battle would never fight with just part of his armor. He needs every piece to defend and protect himself from the onslaught of the enemy. In the same way, if we are to have relentless faith, we need to be warriors who apply the armor day in and day out, so we can stand firm as Scripture suggests.

Ephesians 6:10–17 states the necessary pieces we need to fight the battle. List them and then fill them in on the drawing. Beside each piece of armor, make a note of what it protects or the purpose of the piece of armor as it may relate to us as believers.

FIELDNOTES

I hope you have seen through the power of God's Word that Satan is a genuine enemy to Christ's followers; however, he is not our conqueror! Satan is not all-knowing and can't be everywhere at all times. He is a created being, a fallen angel, and his power is limited. The victory was won on the cross; Jesus paid the price for us by His shed blood, which broke the chains of hell and death. But that doesn't mean the devil stops trying to accuse us before the Father or stops throwing arrows in an attempt to discourage or defeat us with despair. He is the father of lies and, as we have learned, he is out for revenge to discredit us because he knows the sand in his hourglass has almost run out, and the time for judgment and hell is near.

Review the image of armor. Which piece(s) have you forgotten to put on lately? Ask God to help you remember to fight for your faith daily by accessing the armor.

Leprous Pride

We now enter the story of Uzziah's life at a tragic point in the narrative. It only takes a few sentences to find out the reason that led to his downfall. After we learn of all that he did to prepare his army for battle and the success God gave him, the tables turn, and we find Uzziah, much like his father, Amaziah, choosing not to listen.

Read 2 Kings 15:5 and 2 Chronicles 26:15–20.

What is missing in the account from 2 Kings 15? Okay, scribes let's write out these significant verses from 2 Chronicles 26:15–20 in your notebook or journal.

Review what you've written and highlight the reasons for Uzziah's downfall. Make a list of the sequence you observe from the text.

This is a gut-wrenching part of the story because Uzziah was doing so well. It isn't clear in what part of his reign he decided to enter the temple's inner sanctuary. We can speculate that it happened toward the latter part since his son Jotham was co-regent and carried out the king's duties before he ascended to the throne at the age of twenty-five after his father's death.[7]

We might ask, how could Uzziah, after all the success and blessing God gave him, blow it so badly? Why would he defy not just one priest, Azariah, but eighty more priests and push past them and defy the holy law?

The crucial statement "but when he was strong, he grew proud, to his destruction" (2 Chron. 26:16) answers those questions. It has been said that people can change overnight, but I am not sure I agree. It's the series of small compromises that add up until we decide to take God off the throne and do things our way.

In verse 16, the word "grew" is the point at the juncture when Uzziah decided he didn't need God's help any longer. When he *grew* strong, he became arrogant, and when he *grew* arrogant, he turned his face from giving God the glory and took it for himself. So much so that he thought he could overwrite the sacred law and act on his own behalf.

Look at 2 Chronicles 26:17–8. Describe what happened from the priest's perspective.

What characteristics does Scripture use to describe the priests?

Reread verse 19. What was King Uzziah's response? Why was he so angry?

Pride and anger feed off each other, and we see this with Uzziah. His pride fueled his rage, and at that point, there was no turning back because his heart was full of arrogance. He was miffed that the eighty-one brave priests tried to hold him accountable. When pride reaches this level in a person's life, it's hard to listen because, at this place, everyone else is inferior, and the proud person is superior.

God judged not only Uzziah's act of rebellion, but the intent in his heart and his pride. Stepping outside of the fear of God became Uzziah's undoing, and God is clear about how He feels about pride.

Look up the following verses on pride. Then summarize your findings.

Proverbs 8:13

Proverbs 11:2

Proverbs 13:10

Proverbs 26:12

Proverbs 29:23

Psalm 10:4

James 4:6

Summary:

What did you learn about humility from these verses?

Write definitions of pride and humility. Compare and contrast both below.

PRIDE	HUMILITY

This is a lesson that I don't think any of us want to learn the way Uzziah learned. We might say that God's response was harsh, but in contrast, Uzziah's single act of pride had several implications. First, he was the king, and part of his responsibility was "to protect and uphold the temple and its institutions."[8]

Second, he showed his disregard in fearing the Lord. He appointed himself priest and king. Perhaps, as C. Knapp suggests in his book *Kings of Judah,* it's possible Uzziah wanted to follow the Egyptian kings by combining the office of king and high priest to hold religious and civil powers.[9] It wasn't enough that God had given him success and fame throughout the region. His hunger for more power led to his heart hardening with pride, which ultimately led to the black stain on his reputation at the end of his life. That was how he was remembered at the end of his reign, but also as a godly king.

Finish out the study of Uzziah's life by reading 2 Chronicles 26:21–22.

How was he forced to live out the rest of his days? List his restrictions.

What did he have to give up as king as a result of his sin?

FIELDNOTES

This is a sobering account and scares me to death. And before you and I think that we are not capable of something similar, we need to fall to our knees and confess that we too can open the door to pride if we aren't careful. Faithful living means being consistent in inviting God to speak and then responding in obedience.

May we be women of humility and catch those moments of pride before they *grow* into disobedience. As we close our time together, sit in God's presence and ask Him if there is any pride lurking in your heart. Sit long enough for Him to reveal His truth through the Holy Spirit.

Jotham
The King Who Stayed Out of the Inner Temple

Jotham's reign, for the most part, was uneventful. Before he took the throne, Jotham ruled alongside his father, King Uzziah, until the end of Uzziah's life. He followed in his father's footsteps, except for violating the command not to enter the inner sanctum of the temple. The season of ruling alongside his father most likely served as a daily reminder of seeing his father's diseased condition. It was a visual reminder and warning against defiling the holy temple and God's directives.

SURVEY

Reread 2 Kings 15:32–36 and read 2 Chronicles 27:1–2.

Let's begin today by completing the Judah Regnal Formula in order to study the background of Jotham.

JUDAH REGNAL FORMULA: KING JOTHAM

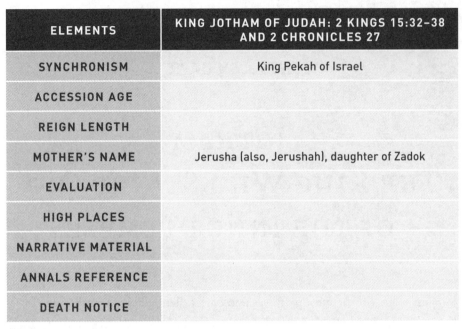

ELEMENTS	KING JOTHAM OF JUDAH: 2 KINGS 15:32-38 AND 2 CHRONICLES 27
SYNCHRONISM	King Pekah of Israel
ACCESSION AGE	
REIGN LENGTH	
MOTHER'S NAME	Jerusha (also, Jerushah), daughter of Zadok
EVALUATION	
HIGH PLACES	
NARRATIVE MATERIAL	
ANNALS REFERENCE	
DEATH NOTICE	

Read 2 Chronicles 27:3–9. *Again, while 2 Kings dedicates a few verses to Jotham's reign, 2 Chronicles 27 more completely outlines his sixteen-year reign. Note below what you observe from verses 3–9, including his accomplishments.*

What does verse 6 say about Jotham?

Describe what it means to not waver in obeying God.

We have this commentary about King Jotham in 2 Chronicles 27, but look back at verse 2. Why do you think the people still behaved corruptly? How does that reflect on King Jotham, or does it?

EXCAVATE

When we think about Jotham's reign, spiritual revival doesn't seem to be a major theme. However, he accomplished repairing the temple and taking on some significant building projects around Judah. He even subdued the Ammonites, and they paid tribute to Judah for several years, strengthening Judah's economic position. Jotham didn't follow in his father's footsteps by dishonoring the Lord, but idolatry still had a firm hold on Judah. The evaluation Scripture that he was obedient to God throughout his reign—despite the grip idolatry had on Judah—speaks to his faithfulness to follow God.

Review the regnal formulas for Jotham's father, Uzziah, and grandfather, Amaziah. How far back do you think idolatry had a hold on Judah?

FIELDNOTES

There has been so much to think about for this week's study. We've looked at what it means to be prepared for the battle and guarding our hearts against pride. We've learned how seriously God takes our sin and disobedience. All these are critical to building relentless faith in our lives. Take a few moments to thank God for His grace and faithfulness.

Write down three ways you can decide to guard your heart against pride this coming week. And then read Ephesians 6:10–18 out loud.

Write it out as a prayer as you close your study for this week.

PRAYER

Dear God . . .

Know Your Enemies

Uzziah had some powerful enemies during his reign: the Philistines, Arabians, and Meunites. He was familiar with the Philistines as his ancestor King Jehoram had fought the Philistines and the Arabians. Jehoram, who you'll remember was married to Athaliah (Ahab's daughter), walked in the ways of the house of Ahab. Because of his idolatry, the Bible says: "And the LORD stirred up against Jehoram the anger of the Philistines and of the Arabians who are near the Ethiopians" (2 Chron. 21:16). And to add grief to misery, they plundered his possessions, including his sons and his wives, except for his youngest son.

The Philistines were a fierce enemy and were constantly on the heels of the Hebrews. You may remember reading about King Saul fighting the Philistines (1 Sam. 13) and a young David slaying the Philistine giant, Goliath (1 Sam. 17:38–52).

The Philistines' method of warfare was that they held the tribes, especially the southern tribes, in degrading servitude (Judg. 15:11; 1 Sam. 13:19–22); at other times they were defeated in great slaughter (1 Sam. 14:1–47; 17).[10]

This may have been Uzziah's motivation to reclaim what had been taken in previous generations. God gave him success because "He set himself to seek God in the days of Zechariah, who instructed him in the fear of God, and as long as he sought the LORD, God made him prosper" (2 Chron. 26:5).

This was the absolute opposite of King Jehoram, and Uzziah was determined to take this enemy with God's help. He built cities in the conquered territories and subdued their influence.

The Arabians are the same nation who paid tribute to Solomon (2 Chron. 9:14) and to Jehoshaphat (2 Chron. 17:11). In early Hebrew history, the Arabians were known as the "Ishmaelites, descendants of Keturah."[11] A tribute could be imposed upon a nation by a conquering nation. This was to keep them under control and make sure they didn't revolt and make war against them. Tributes were paid in the form of currency, such as gold or silver and treasures from a kingdom. The Assyrians, another feared enemy, often kept nations in check by making them pay vast amounts of tribute to keep them from invading the kingdom, so the Assyrians could live in freedom. Often tributes could bankrupt a nation, causing them to lose their ability to prosper.

The Meunites were also an Arab tribe that lived on the border of Judah. Because Uzziah had conquered them, they paid a tax to Uzziah during his reign.[12] We learn from his reign that he was intentional about subduing his enemies. In the same way, we can't just sit around and be naïve, thinking the enemy isn't going to bother us. Like Uzziah, we have to go out and be prepared to face our enemy, and with God's help subdue our enemy so we can live in freedom and victory!

One of the ways to be intentional is to suit up every day and put on our armor. Write out Ephesians 6:10–18 in your notebook or journal as a prayer to intentionally stand against the enemy. Personalize it for your situation and add other Scriptures if needed. Make it a declaration when you are tempted to doubt; believe that God will help you.

King Hezekiah

REFORMING PRAYER

Jehovah is my strength[1]

"And he did what was right in the eyes of the LORD,
according to all that David his father had done. . . . He trusted in the LORD,
the God of Israel, so that there was none like him among all the kings
of Judah after him, nor among those who were before him."
2 KINGS 18:3, 5

When our boys were in elementary and middle school, we went on what we called the Cavanaugh Heritage Trip. We traced both sides of the family, first in Germany and the surrounding countries, and then made our way to the UK, where we visited England, Scotland, Wales, and finally traced the history of our surname, Cavanaugh, in Ireland.

Our bed-and-breakfast had a charming host who gathered us together in her parlor to tell the boys a story. The Irish love to talk about their history and are marvelous storytellers. The boys sat on her sofa, wide-eyed and mesmerized by the lilt of her Irish brogue as she proceeded to share with us that the Cavanaugh Clan came from a long line of noble warriors who fought bravely against the enemies attempting to conquer Ireland's lands.

She mentioned that there were some Cavanaugh castles in the area, so we set out on a quest to see these noble places of our ancestors. Maps in hand, we all piled into our rental car to see our first castle. When we arrived, we were more than disappointed; we were devastated at what lay before our eyes: a castle in ruins with no roof, missing walls, and moss and grass growing in and around the aged, rough-hewn blocks that at one time made a mighty fortress. The previous day, we had imagined defenses well preserved with banners and worn battle shields that would tell us more about our heritage. Instead, we saw the noble homestead of our ancestors lying in ruins.

This reminds me of where we are headed this week in our study of King Hezekiah. Hezekiah was the grandson of King Jotham. Hezekiah's father, Ahaz, ruled in between these two godly kings. You might want to refresh your memory and refer to the Kings Genealogy Timeline in the back of the book. Unlike his grandfather, Jotham, who inherited the throne when Judah was prosperous and economically sound because of his father King Uzziah, Hezekiah inherited a kingdom nearly in ruin following the sixteen-year reign of his father, King Ahaz.

Idolatry, child sacrifice, pagan altars on every corner in Jerusalem, and alliances with the surrounding nations were only a few of Ahaz's evil deeds. Compared to everything Uzziah had accomplished, Ahaz was a spiritual and economic wrecking ball. The country was in bondage to neighboring nations. The holy temple was desecrated with altars to foreign gods, and Ahaz closed and shut God's holy temple down tight. The people had never been so idolatrous.

In Isaiah chapter 1, the prophet gives a visual picture of how wicked Judah had become. *The Moody Bible Commentary* says that King Ahaz was "'one of the weakest and most corrupt of all the twenty rulers in Judah.'"[2]

King Hezekiah takes center stage, the polar opposite of his father. In his first hundred days after ascending to the throne, Hezekiah opens the Lord's temple and repairs the damage. He gathers the priests and begins a national reform to lead the people back to worshiping Jehovah. The reforms and conquests of Hezekiah cover seven chapters between Kings and Chronicles, so we have our work cut out for us this week. Gather up your biblical archaeological tools, and ask the Holy Spirit to open our eyes and our hearts.

This week we are going to be studying the fifth pillar of faithful living for lasting influence—***Reforming Prayer.*** Are you ready? We're about to explore and follow the path of Hezekiah's leadership to bring God back to the center of Judah.

A Timeline of Hezekiah's Reign

There is an enormous amount to cover in Scripture with King Hezekiah, so we will break down the study in bite-sized chunks. However, for our first day, I want you to grasp an overview of his reign. There are ninety-five verses over the span of three chapters that should take you about thirty minutes to read. You'll need to have the full context before using your sharp skills and tools to extract the treasures the Holy Spirit is waiting to give. Grab your favorite java or tea and get cozy with your Bible.

Read 2 Kings 18–20. *As you read, make some observations about Hezekiah's journey.*

Drawing from the observations you noted on 2 Kings chapters 18, 19, and 20, fill in the Regnal Formula for Hezekiah.

JUDAH REGNAL FORMULA: KING HEZEKIAH

ELEMENTS	KING HEZEKIAH OF JUDAH: 2 KINGS 18–20 AND 2 CHRONICLES 29–32
SYNCHRONISM	King Hoshea of Israel
ACCESSION AGE	
REIGN LENGTH	
MOTHER'S NAME	
EVALUATION	
HIGH PLACES	
NARRATIVE MATERIAL	
ANNALS REFERENCE	
DEATH NOTICE	

EXCAVATE

The books of Kings and Chronicles offer us more information for our biblical archaeological dig than we have days for this week. Yet, I hope and pray that God will help you lift out from the Scriptures the most significant truths as we focus on the pillar of *Reforming Prayer*.

Looking over your notes and observations, write a brief description of the life of Hezekiah. Maybe this will inspire you: If you had to write a social media profile to introduce Hezekiah, what would you say?

FIELDNOTES

I'm incredibly proud of you! Soaking up this much narrative is a big task and yet critical to seeing the bigger picture. We covered a large portion of Scripture today, but I promise we will bring the pieces together as we move through the rest of the week.

As you reflect on your reading, what is one truth that stands out above the rest? Write it down and take some time to pray over it as we close Day One of our study.

REFORMS AND RESTORATION

It's hard to imagine the cleanup job Hezekiah had before him of restoring the temple worship his father Ahaz had devastated, both physically and spiritually. To understand the scope of what Hezekiah was facing, we need to explore the mess he stepped into when he became king.

Scripture tells us that from the beginning, his father, King Ahaz, was in a spiritual downward spiral. The problems that consequently arose because of his actions didn't drive him to God; instead, they drove him further into evil. Chronicles says, "In the time of his distress he became yet more faithless to the Lord" (2 Chron. 28:22). All Ahaz's attempts to be free from his enemies, such as adopting their worship, building altars, and paying tribute to Assyria, didn't help him (2 Chron. 28:21). He fell further and further into wickedness, dragging Judah along with him into a state of spiritual bankruptcy and financial ruin.

SURVEY

Read 2 Kings 16:10–17.

Ahaz's visit to the king of Assyria, Tiglath-pileser, only further entrenched his desire for idolatry. He admired the pattern of their pagan altar and, returning home, proceeded to build a model of what he saw in Damascus.

Make a list of all that Ahaz did after he returned from Damascus.

Who was his accomplice in these wicked acts? How do you suppose Uriah the priest came to stoop to carrying out Ahaz's wishes?

Read 2 Chronicles 28:23–25. *What do these verses say about King Ahaz's reasons for his acts?*

In contrast, let's look at how Hezekiah approached the mess that his father made.

Read 2 Chronicles 29:3–8. *What is the first thing Hezekiah did?*

What did he say to the priests?

Look up the word "consecrate" in a concordance. Write the definition.

How does this apply to us as modern-day believers? How are we to consecrate ourselves?

Read 2 Chronicles 29:16–19. *Make a list of what the priests had to do to clean up the temple.*

After they were finished, what did they tell Hezekiah in verses 18 and 19? Why do you think this was so significant to restoring the temple worship?

In 2 Chronicles chapters 29 and 30, we find that Hezekiah repairs the temple and organizes the priests to lead the people in worship. He also carried out the traditional Hebrew rituals of worship and all that God commanded His people to do. In addition, he restored the Passover, which hadn't been celebrated in Jerusalem for generations.

EXCAVATE

Author Lynn Austin has written a series of historical fiction books called The Chronicles of the Kings.[3] Well-researched, both biblically and historically, this series depicts the lives of the kings. In the opening chapter of her narrative on Hezekiah, Austin paints strong imagery of the incredible devastation that resulted from the practice of child sacrifice and idol worship in Judah.

Living with a corrupt and vile father must have made a lasting impact on Hezekiah as he grew up. He could have been traumatized as a child, knowing that one or more of his siblings had been sacrificed and offered to the Canaanite god Molech, the idol Ahaz had set up in the Valley of Hinnom. "He even burned his son as an offering, according to the despicable practices of the nations whom the LORD drove out before the people of Israel" (2 Kings 16:3). This possibly scarred Hezekiah emotionally and perhaps was the motivation for him to be a different kind of ruler.

Can you see why God was provoked to anger and that His heart was broken because Judah turned away from their true worship of Jehovah under King Ahaz? When I picture King Ahaz shutting the doors of the house of the Lord, I shudder with grief. He cut off every possible route for God's people to repent and worship. Hezekiah, in contrast, made worship of Jehovah the priority when he became king. He knew that if the people's hearts were aligned with God, then the rest would follow faithful living.

The same holds true for us: when our worship of God is a priority, then the rest of our life will be one of faithfulness and lasting influence. As I was praying this week for which truth we could focus on for our study of Hezekiah, God reminded me how I tend to shut the doors of my worship with Him when I am in pain. The hurt causes me to run away instead of running to Him. I am still figuring out the reasons why, at times, I'm tempted to run. I am learning to not overthink it too much, as He has given me a significant victory in recent years. Likewise, we all have a choice when we suffer and go through hard seasons. They can either cause us to draw closer to Jesus or push Him away.

Hezekiah could have easily turned and followed in his father's footsteps and continued walking in evil ways, or created his own method of worship, hiding his pain in silence. His story gives us hope when the generation before us has paved a path of ungodliness and hurt others in the process.

Read the following verses. What does each tell you about God's promise to you when you are in a tough season but are encouraged to worship and praise?

Psalm 16:7–8

Psalm 59:16–17

Isaiah 43:2

Isaiah 57:15–16

Habakkuk 3:17–19

Romans 4:20

2 Corinthians 1:3

James 1:12

Hezekiah most likely had deep wounds from a destructive father and yet he turned his pain into worship and prayer and it resulted in a reformation of Judah. His decision to put God at the center not only brought healing to his soul, but to the nation. You might be a victim of someone else's sinful choices, which were totally out of your control. You may be tempted to shut down or run. Can I encourage you? Don't let the pain and wounds cause you to close the doors on your relationship with Jesus. Talk to Him—He's waiting to sit with you and listen.

Please don't let the sins of someone else snuff out your light. Allow God to use your pain as a catalyst to live out His promises with faith and courage. Those closest to you are watching to see if your faith matches your actions in the tough times. Perfection isn't the goal; just take one faithful step at a time, bringing your sacrifice of praise with thanksgiving in worship and prayer.

Is there some hidden pain in your life that keeps you from opening the doors to worship? What damage needs to be repaired?

What is one small step you can take this week to restore prayer?

WORSHIP AND MIRACLES

As king, Hezekiah's political position was one of debt as a tributary to Assyria. Previously, King Ahaz had voluntarily made himself a servant of Tiglath-pileser king of Assyria, in exchange for his help against the king of Syria. A new king being on the throne didn't cancel the debt. Unfortunately, the heir would be in bondage to pay tribute. This is what Hezekiah inherited. And the only way to free himself from paying tribute would be to revolt against Assyria. This would bring severe consequences, as the Assyrians were a dominant power in the ancient Near East (modern-day Iraq).

Assyria was one of the most-feared nations during that time in history. Along with a siege type of warfare, they also used psychological warfare by torturing captured soldiers. One gruesome act involved impaling or flaying their captives and positioning the bodies around the city to be conquered in order to terrorize their enemies into submission.[4] Their brutality in their conquests of other nations was well-known, and anyone who dared revolt paid a high price.[5] Many a city surrendered when it heard the Assyrian army was coming to take their city.

Now we find Hezekiah up against a most challenging scenario: facing down King Sennacherib from Assyria. "After these things and these acts of faithfulness, Sennacherib king of Assyria came and invaded Judah and encamped against the fortified cities, thinking to win them for himself" (2 Chron. 32:1).

Read 2 Chronicles 32:1–8.

What does Hezekiah do when he finds out that he is being invaded by Assyria?

How does he encourage the citizens of Jerusalem? (v. 7)

How did the people respond?

Do you think this was a result of trust being rebuilt from restoring the worship? Why or why not?

Since they were camped around Jerusalem but had not yet taken it, the Assyrians resorted to pillaging neighboring towns as a sign of what they might do to Jerusalem. They taunted and mocked Jehovah God in hopes that the people would surrender.

Read the account in 2 Kings 18:13–16.

What did Hezekiah do to preserve Jerusalem?

Why do you think he did this?

Read verses 9–12. What happened?

Why do you suppose Hezekiah told the Assyrian king that he (Hezekiah) had done wrong? What was his strategy?

The slaughter and capture of the northern kingdom of Israel was fresh in Hezekiah's mind. The Assyrians had carried off their brothers from Israel, and it was the final end of the northern kingdom, once part of the divided kingdom.

Reread verses 10–15, and list the reasons why God allowed the north (Israel) to be taken into captivity.

The king of Assyria sent an entourage and his most polished orator, his Rabshakeh (a title rather than a name). A Rabshakeh could speak Hebrew in order to relay a message to the people of Judah, not once but twice—first verbally, and then in letters to the king.

Read 2 Chronicles 32:10–18 and 2 Kings 19:10–13.

How is the Rabshakeh mocking and manipulating the people of Judah in both accounts?

Are the letters effective? (To read the complete account you can also reread 2 Kings 19:1–36).

Reread Hezekiah's desperate prayer in 2 Kings 19:14–19. What does he ask of the Lord? Write out his prayer in your notebook or journal.

After Hezekiah prayed, the prophet came to give Hezekiah a message from God in answer to his prayers. The prophet assures him of victory against the mighty enemy of Assyria. He lets him know that the enemy won't set foot in the city, and the people of Jerusalem won't even see an arrow or weapon against them. God says, "For I will defend this city to save it, for my own sake and the sake of my servant David" (2 Kings 19:34).

Notice that God says, "for my own sake." What do you think is meant by this statement?

The miracle victory happens in 2 Kings 19:35–36. How does God deliver them from their enemy?

Read 2 Chronicles 32:22–23. *What else happened as a result of the triumph?*

EXCAVATE

Faithful living is living a life of prayer. Hezekiah was prepared to face the battle because his heart was ready; he made prayer and worship a priority. He could kneel before the altar of God with a distressing letter from his enemy and have confidence that God would hear his prayers because he lived a life of worship. He knew he was a human being with limitations and no comparison to a Holy God.

God came to Hezekiah through the prophet Isaiah to reassure him that God was in control, and He would act on his behalf. We all need reassurance when we encounter a life situation like a letter from our enemy, just as King Hezekiah had a strong voice of truth in his life through Isaiah.

Who is your voice of truth when you need it most? Who reminds you that God hasn't forgotten or abandoned you, and who promises to help you?

FIELDNOTES

Faithful living doesn't always mean agreeing with others. Many times, God calls us to be faithful in circumstances that others just shake their head at and wonder: *How can you continue in such chaos? Make a decision already!* I am sure that King Hezekiah heard voices that urged him to surrender to the Assyrian king. Instead, he listened to God and let God fight the battle for him, experiencing a far greater result than if he would have surrendered to the enemy. The city of Jerusalem was spared, and the people of Judah were able to live in peace.

There are times when it feels like our enemy, the devil, is like the Rabshakeh screaming from outside our walls, hurling insults, and manipulating our vulnerability. His goal is to have us give up and trust in our own truth instead of the truth of God's character.

Are you standing on a wall like Hezekiah with his leaders and listening to a Rabshakeh trying to deliver a message of defeat in your life?

What do you know to be true right now in your current circumstance? Fill in the chart below:

CURRENT SITUATION	"RABSHAKEH" LIES	GOD'S TRUTH

Last, ask the hard question. Ask God to show you if you are a Rabshakeh in someone else's life. If you are, repent, asking God to help you release control and bless the other person.

PRAYER CHANGES THINGS

We see a pattern in Hezekiah's life. When he is in distress, he prays. He knows where to go for help. Unlike his ancestor King Asa who refused to ask God for help when he was sick, Hezekiah immediately entered into prayer after Isaiah visited him with the disturbing message.

Reread 2 Kings 20:1–11.

List your observations.

What is Hezekiah's state?

Why do you think the Scripture said he wept bitterly?

We might conclude that one of the main reasons he was so distraught is because he had no heir. Later in Scripture, we find that he has a son, Manasseh, who is twelve years old when he takes the throne. And because of God's merciful response in granting Hezekiah another fifteen years to live, we can deduce that he became a father three years after he recovered from his illness.

SURVEY

Read Isaiah 38:9–20.

Hezekiah's account of his illness excludes a prayer in our reading of 2 Kings that we find recorded instead in the book of Isaiah.

What do you find is Hezekiah's common thread in this prayer?

What is his hope?

What is his promise of thanksgiving to God?

EXCAVATE

What we find here is nothing short of amazing in that God extends Hezekiah's life. Does this give you hope for your current problem, that God can be reached by prayer? It should because God loves to give good gifts to His children.

Read James 1:17–18 and Matthew 7:7–11. *What do these passages say about God's gifts? What gift do you need from God?*

Read Psalm 18:6. *What promise is found in this verse about prayer?*

FIELDNOTES

When have you prayed and seen God answer your prayer in ways you never imagined? What happened?

Write out a prayer of thanksgiving in response to God's answer.

Fools of the Future

Every king has a final chapter that speaks to what he passes on to the next generation. It seems that even after God graciously granted Hezekiah's prayer, Hezekiah walked right into making a foolish decision and left his future generations vulnerable and exposed.

Summarize 2 Chronicles 32:27–31 as if you were a journalist writing a lead story for the local newspaper. What would be your headline?

SURVEY

Read 2 Kings 20:14–18.

After Hezekiah foolishly exposed the wealth of his kingdom to the Babylonian envoy, Isaiah paid him a visit.

What did Isaiah warn Hezekiah about?

What was the reason Hezekiah said he showed the Babylonians everything?

Look now in 2 Chronicles for clues to answer the above questions. Make observations about verses 32:23, 25–27.

Verse 31 says, "God left him to himself, in order to test him and to know all that was in his heart."

How does Hezekiah's response to Isaiah reveal what was in his heart in 2 Kings 20:19?

EXCAVATE

Living a life of reforming prayer for lasting influence means we care about future generations. We are aware of how the decisions and choices we make today will impact our loved ones tomorrow, next month, next year, and in the decades to follow. It is evident by Hezekiah's response that he was okay with what he did as long as the consequence didn't impact him. He would have peace, and that is all that mattered to him. Is that all that matters to us? That the consequences of our actions only affect us? What about our children and our children's children, and their children? Or if you don't have children, what about those in your sphere of influence as an aunt, mentor, or teacher? Here is a sobering truth: what you decide in a series of moments has a lasting impact on future generations. What might you be doing right now that you need to correct? Ask God to help you live in greater faithfulness.

As we wrap up this week's study, I want to circle back to where we began with the start of Hezekiah's reign and share a family story. Our eldest son Jeremy was barely two years old, and our little family had been through a tough season. We moved two states away and found ourselves struggling to make ends meet. We didn't know if we would have enough money for groceries or rent for the month.

This move put many strains on our family life. I was extremely overwhelmed. One day I was in the kitchen doing dishes and struggling with discouragement. From around the corner, Jeremy called to me in our small townhouse. I found him sitting on the stairs raising his hands in worship. In his sweet two-year-old voice he said, "Mommy, come sit with me and praise the Lord." He patted the space next to him on the step and repeated his request about three times.

I hesitated for a moment because I wondered who he had seen expressing worship by the raising of hands. We attended a conservative church where that expression made people uncomfortable. With tears in my eyes, I sat next to him.

He repeated his request once again, "Mommy, praise the Lord with me."

As I lifted my hands in praise and worship, I sensed God reaching down through the worship of my son. God whispered to me that my heart was teetering on the brink of making a crucial choice that would impact my son and our family. Would I allow my discouragement and defeat to lead me away from God instead of allowing Him to hold my heart and to trust Him with our circumstances? *Trust Me*, are the words I heard through my young son's worship. Later that day, I confessed my discouragement and my sin of unbelief. I surrendered, and then I worshiped once again.

This reminds me of what takes place before a victory: worship and prayer. That's what we have studied this week and learned from Hezekiah. When this king was in distress, he prayed, and he worshiped. Worship was his priority, and he restored the temple worship immediately. He "put God back" in His rightful place in Judah and declared to Jerusalem and all the regions of Judah that God gave him victory. God delivered them from the vast and powerful Assyrian army (2 Chron. 32:20–23) and from a human perspective their situation was hopeless. But God sent His angel armies and defeated the enemy. May we be like Hezekiah and worship even in the midst of our pain, woundedness, hurt, and despair.

Take an honest assessment of your prayer and worship. Are you choosing to worship and pray even in the middle of your mess? Why or why not?

Name your worry and your concern in a written prayer below. Then lift up your heart in worship and prayer.

PRAYER

Dear God . . .

Praying in Distress

Hezekiah faced impossible odds when the King of Assyria besieged Judah:

> Then Hezekiah the king and Isaiah the prophet, the son of Amoz, prayed
> because of this and cried to heaven. And the LORD sent an angel, who cut
> off all the mighty warriors and commanders and officers in the camp of
> the king of Assyria. So he returned with shame of face to his own land.
> (2 Chron. 32:20–21)

This is a prayer of severe distress, as we learned in our study this past week. King
Hezekiah wasn't alone; other kings prayed desperate prayers when facing similar
circumstances. One of my favorites is King Jehoshaphat several generations earlier
(2 Chron. 20). He was facing a similar scenario of enemies coming against the
land of Judah. He immediately cried out to the Lord, proclaimed a fast, and gathered the people of Judah together from near and far to seek the Lord. He prayed
a passionate prayer reminding God of His power and faithfulness. He ended his
prayer with, "O our God, will you not execute judgment on them? For we are
powerless against this great horde that is coming against us. We do not know what
to do, but our eyes are on you" (v. 12).

God sent a message through Jahaziel (v. 14) and reminded King Jehoshaphat and
all who were listening that God would fight this battle; they were only to be still
and watch and see the deliverance of the Lord (v.16–17). And God was faithful
to answer exactly as He promised. God answered and gave them a victory so great
that it took them three days to carry off the loot from their enemies (v. 25). After
this, they gathered and blessed the Lord and returned "to Jerusalem with joy."
(v. 27).

There is a surefire pattern for seeking the Lord as Jehoshaphat did that we can adopt when we are in distress:

1. Fast and pray (v. 3)

2. Recount God's faithfulness—remember (vv. 6–12)

3. Don't be afraid or discouraged (v.15)

4. Position yourselves, stand still, and see the salvation of the Lord (v. 17)

5. Worship (v.18)

6. Give thanks and praise (vv. 21–22)

Jehoshaphat and all of Judah (southern kingdom) applied all these steps before they received their deliverance. After they praised God, Jehoshaphat led them out into the wilderness of Tekoa. The King declared, "Hear me, Judah and inhabitants of Jerusalem! Believe in the LORD your God, and you will be established; believe his prophets, and you will succeed" (v. 20).

Their faith infused their courage, and they began to sing and praise. At that moment with their voices lifted high, exalting Jehovah, God set an ambush that defeated their enemies (v. 22).

The next time you face a desperate situation, model this pattern of prayer and watch and see how God answers!

KING JOSIAH

REBUILDING WORSHIP

Whom Jehovah Heals[1]

"And he did what was right in the eyes of the LORD and walked in all the way of
David his father, and he did not turn aside to the right or to the left."
2 KINGS 22:2

Can you believe it? We are nearly at the finish line studying our last godly king,
and I absolutely love that we can finish *The Godly Kings of Judah* with King Josiah.
From the time he took the throne as a child, and throughout his reign, he had
a tender heart toward God. He didn't stray or betray Jehovah. He, like Asa and
Hezekiah, swept up the mess from the previous generations. And King Josiah
had a lot of sweeping up to do as his father, King Amon, and grandfather, King
Manasseh, had kept Judah in idolatrous bondage.

Before we look at King Josiah, let's take a closer look at his grandfather, King
Manasseh, who is listed as a wicked king. Unlike his counterparts in both Israel
and Judah, Manasseh chooses to repent at the end of his reign. I don't want to skip

over the significance of his repentance because it holds wisdom for us to consider as we talk about faithful living for lasting influence. In the first half of the week, we will peek into Manasseh's reign; then in the latter part of the week, we will contrast his life with King Josiah's.

MANASSEH'S DESTRUCTION

It's hard to fathom that Manasseh walked clearly in the opposite direction of the leadership of his father, King Hezekiah. He reversed all the reforms his father did to restore Judah's worship of Jehovah. Manasseh was the longest reigning king (fifty-five years) in the southern kingdom of Judah. His actions were not only destructive but led Judah into more darkness and evil than the pagan nations God drove out from Israel (2 Kings 21:2, 11). Manasseh was just twelve years old when he began his reign and we can assume that his father the king had died shortly before.

Losing your father at the tender age of twelve would be devastating. Scripture doesn't give the backstory but we can speculate how his deep loss might have impacted his ability to follow in the footsteps of King Hezekiah's reforms. We will never know the reasons why he chose the path of evil, but there is a glimmer of hope in his story that we will uncover as we begin this week's study.

Read 2 Kings 21:1–18.

What facts do you note about King Manasseh? (vv. 1–3)

What did he rebuild?

The great nineteenth-century preacher Charles Spurgeon made this observation about Manasseh:

> He was a very glutton for iniquity, so he fraternized with the devil by
> seeking after all kinds of supernatural witcheries and wizardries. He
> seemed as if he could not get far enough away from God. Everything that
> was forbidden appeared just suited to his depraved taste, and if he must
> not do it, why, then he resolved that he would do it![2]

Look up the following Scriptures and fill out the chart below listing the acts God says are abominations. The Hebrew word for "abomination" is *toebah* and simply means "something disgusting, an abhorrence, to loathe and detest."[3]

Next to the verses, reference your reading in 2 Kings 21:1–18; if necessary, refer to 2 Chronicles 33:1–9 to fill in the gaps.

ABOMINATIONS TO GOD	MANASSEH'S ACTS
DEUTERONOMY 4:19	
DEUTERONOMY 12:31	
DEUTERONOMY 16:21	
DEUTERONOMY 18:9–12	
ISAIAH 2:6	
JEREMIAH 14:14	
LEVITICUS 19:31; 20:6, 27	
ISAIAH 8:19	

You might have discovered a new word as I did when I studied this list of Manasseh's sins—necromancy. A necromancer practices divination by conjuring up the dead. This was the downfall of the first king of Israel, Saul (see 1 Sam. 28). When he was up against the Philistines, he didn't wait to hear from God; instead, he went to a necromancer, and the medium of En-dor did as Saul requested by "bringing up" Samuel the prophet. Saul didn't receive the news he wanted, only the judgment that God had rejected him because of his disobedience and that his enemy would defeat him.

From your observations in the chart, was there any evil that Manasseh didn't practice?

Read 2 Kings 21:9. *What did God say about him?*

What didn't the Israelites and Manasseh listen to? (v. 8).

EXCAVATE

Our study reveals that this isn't the first time such idolatries and practices are mentioned. In fact, there are numerous times in the books of Kings and Chronicles that these practices occurred. And yet God is merciful time and time again, giving the kings and the people chance after chance.

Before we too quickly shudder over Manasseh's evil, we need to ask ourselves if there are any contemporary forms of these types of idolatry in our life.

What does idolatry look like today in our culture? In the church culture?

I can't emphasize enough the importance of God's Word in our lives. This week our sixth pillar of faithful living for lasting influence is **Rebuilding Worship.** Continually renewing ourselves in God's Word is critical for faithful living. It is His Word that keeps us from falling into habitual sin and heading down a dark path of deception, which in turn becomes idolatry. The Word also helps to strengthen our spirit to discern and recognize false truth when it knocks on our door. Our sword (Eph. 6:17) is our weapon to fight against the evil one who seeks to turn us away from God.

What do Hebrews 4:12 and 2 Timothy 3:16 tell us about the Word of God?

How can knowing God's Word help us keep from practicing idolatry?

FIELDNOTES

When I was preparing to write this study, it became evident how much our current culture seems to be riding a tidal wave of twisted ideologies that exalt themselves against God. It is more important than ever to know God's Word and be able to exercise discernment through the Holy Spirit's influence, to understand what the Word says so we can recognize when deception invites a little truth and, in turn, becomes half-truth, "a statement that mingles truth and falsehood with deliberate intent to deceive."[4]

Second Timothy 3:1–7 is a warning that reflects our culture today. Read this passage and focus primarily on verse 6. Note your observations.

When you read verse 6, where Timothy refers to women as "weak," let's be careful not to get offended and think, that would never happen to me—being deceived! Let's dig a little deeper. *The Moody Bible Commentary* explains the passage this way:

> The false teachers described were spiritual predators who targeted susceptible women (v. 6). The Greek term translated **weak women** may refer particularly to those who were wealthy and at leisure. False teachers hoped to enrich themselves off their support, and these women, beset by their sins, would grasp at any teaching that offered an escape from their bondage, even if it was false teaching. Those victimized by these teachers (v. 7) were devoted students who never came to the knowledge of the truth. Their root problem was spiritual.[5]

I don't know about you, but this makes me ask some hard questions about myself. Wealth may not necessarily mean money or possessions; how about resources for every problem on the planet? Someone other than God's Spirit can lead us to the many self-help books, podcasts, and courses that promise to fix whatever is wrong or holds us in bondage. Be cautious, be careful, ask the Holy Spirit to help you discern and measure, by God's Word, the truth you are taking in.

Do a little research today or this week before answering the questions. Watch or read the news and record some notes and observations.

Did anything you hear or read remind you of the kingdom of Judah?

What lies are being communicated to our culture?

What is the truth from God's Word?

Where do you see the culture failing?

Matthew 5:13–16 is an encouragement for believers to be salt and light in a dark world. The word "salt" in this passage is precisely what is implied and what we know about salt—that it is a preservative and a symbol of keeping something from spoiling.[6] The world needs your light. It needs you and me to bring the saltiness of the pure gospel truth so we can influence our society.

What can we do practically to be a salty influence? Is there somewhere specific God is asking you to bring salt to our culture?

MANASSEH'S REPENTANCE

Manasseh was so deep into sin he lost the ability to recognize the truth. He had not only set up every type of idolatry that he could find, but he also killed off anyone who confronted him and his practices. Second Kings 21:16 says, "Moreover, Manasseh shed very much innocent blood, till he had filled Jerusalem from one end to another, besides the sin that he made Judah to sin so that they did what was evil in the sight of the LORD."

The visual picture painted here is one of a reign of terror on anyone who might oppose the truth. In *The Kings of Israel and Judah*, George Rawlinson informs us of the darkness of Manasseh:

> But now his conduct took a darker tinge. . . . He set on foot a persecution
> of the adherents of Jehovah and raged against them with all the fierceness
> of an Ahab or an Epiphanes. . . . All the righteous among the Hebrews, says
> Josephus, "did he savagely slay." Among the chief sufferers were those of
> the Prophetical order. "Day by day a fresh batch of them was ordered to ex-
> ecution. . . . It seemed as if a devouring lion were let loosed against them."[7]

Some biblical scholars believe that the aging prophet Isaiah, the voice of truth in Hezekiah's reign, suffered at the hands of Manasseh. Scholars believe it is refer-enced in Hebrews 11:37 as one who was "sawn in two."[8] There is nothing in the Bible that tells us of Isaiah's death or how he died; however, it's highly probable that Isaiah would have been at the top of Manasseh's list.

Finally, God had enough and turned Manasseh over to the king of Assyria.

Read 2 Chronicles 33:9–13.

The rampage of evil takes a 180-degree turn as we find Manasseh humiliated and humbled before his enemies. Time to be the scribe and write verses 9–13 in your notebook or journal.

In the account in Chronicles, how is Manasseh treated?

Manasseh is listed as one of twenty-two princes who paid tribute to Assyria on the Ashurbanipal prism,[9] the annals or records from the Neo-Assyrian period.[10] Historians speculate he may have revolted against paying tribute and was taken to Babylon as punishment.

Such punishment was strategically used by the Assyrians to humiliate the rebel leaders who refused to honor their commitment of tribute. In fact, "captives were sometimes literally led along the road with hooks piercing their lips."[11] As we learned in Week Six, this punishment and other gruesome brutality is the part of Manasseh's narrative that brings him to repentance.

Manasseh's repentance was genuine in that his actions followed (see 2 Chron. 33:14–16). He turned from his wicked ways and sought to restore worship in Judah. He even went as far as to command the people to serve the Lord. All of these acts of obedience were a result of Manasseh choosing to finally listen and obey God even though it took extreme circumstances to put him on the path of repentance.

If you have identified disobedience to God or a message you've closed your ears to, I beg you to put down this study immediately and talk to God about it. Don't let another moment pass without closing the gap in your relationship. Confess your unwillingness to listen and ask God to help you the next time He makes it clear you are to pay attention.

Reread 2 Chronicles 33:10–13. *What does Manasseh do that causes God to have compassion on him?*

Read Psalm 86:15. *What does this verse say about His response to Manasseh? What did God do for him? (2 Chron. 33:13)*

Manasseh's release from being an Assyrian prisoner, would have been highly unusual apart from God's intervention. The Assyrians delighted in making examples of rulers who revolted. The miracle of his release most likely motivated Manasseh to be more than remorseful for his many sins and repent genuinely: "Then Manasseh knew that the LORD was God" (v. 13). God's mercy caused him to act in obedience.

What did he do when he returned to Jerusalem? (2 Chron. 33:14–16)

What does it say about this in verse 17?

Why do you think the people continued to sacrifice to Jehovah on the high places?

EXCAVATE

If you look at 2 Kings 21, you won't find a recording of Manasseh's capture by the king of Assyria or his repentance. There is only the warning in verses 10–15 that God gives and what will occur because of Manasseh's wickedness in turning the hearts of his people against Jehovah. But the fact remains that Manasseh repented, and more than that, God was moved by his prayers.

What does Proverbs 21:1–2 say about God and a king and his heart?

What might repentance look like for us?

Repentance is no small matter and one crucial act that we must learn to practice regularly for faithful living. We looked in depth at the consequences of pride in Week Five.

Look back at Week Five, Day Four and review your answers about pride. How does our pride interfere with repentance?

As we wrap up looking at Manasseh's turnaround and move to Josiah, his grandson, I want to focus on a truth that matters deeply to God. This is for those who feel they have made too many mistakes and been too rebellious for God to hear their prayers. We might even classify our sin as evil and have a story of feeling stuck for years in abusive and addictive behavior that has hurt others. And we might ask how we can possibly live faithful lives and have a lasting influence on our history.

And yet God says we can. He reminds us that His kindness leads us to repentance (Rom. 2:4). Charles Spurgeon explained this further:

> The goodness of God to a person of evil life is not intended to encourage him to continue in his sin but to woo and win him away from it. God manifest his infinite gentleness and love so that he may thereby kill man's sin and win man's hard heart to himself by his tender mercy. God wakens a person's conscience to a sense of his true position in his Maker's sight that he may turn away from the sin he now loves and may seek his God, whom he has despised and neglected.[12]

Read Galatians 5:1. *What does it tell us about what Jesus has done for us when we repent?*

GRACE ABOUNDS

Yesterday was a bit sobering, wasn't it? As I've lived and breathed in these Old Testament narratives for nearly two years in preparation for writing this study, I have been overwhelmed by God's mercy and patience. Can you see it? Over and over again, no matter what His people do, He longs for them to repent and be restored. Manasseh's evil had no limits, and yet studying his story reveals how God still didn't turn His face away when he was in distress. My first thought is, why? He deserved punishment!

I am so glad our God is full of grace. That is what grace means: undeserved favor. And how many times has God been gracious to me when I deserved punishment? Too many times to count. Not only does He give grace, but He says that "He has removed our sins as far from us as the east is from the west" (Ps. 103:12 NLT).

The writer of Chronicles reveals God's gracious character as "God was moved by [Manasseh's] entreaty" (2 Chron. 33:13). Do you know what this means? God hears us when we cry out to Him, and our prayers have the potential to move our Creator God to act. I can hardly wrap my brain around the magnum opus of this truth. It makes me weep to think of how my sin hurts God, and yet He waits for me to come back to Him in obedience. God longs to bless you and me.

We see this in the story of our last king, Josiah.

Reread 2 Kings 22:1–2 and read 2 Chronicles 34:1–6.

We now turn the corner from King Manasseh and breathe in the beauty of a life committed to Jehovah. Complete this final Regnal Formula for King Josiah.

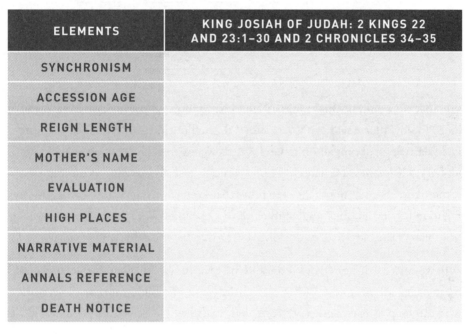

JUDAH REGNAL FORMULA: KING JOSIAH

ELEMENTS	KING JOSIAH OF JUDAH: 2 KINGS 22 AND 23:1–30 AND 2 CHRONICLES 34–35
SYNCHRONISM	
ACCESSION AGE	
REIGN LENGTH	
MOTHER'S NAME	
EVALUATION	
HIGH PLACES	
NARRATIVE MATERIAL	
ANNALS REFERENCE	
DEATH NOTICE	

EXCAVATE

Second Kings 23:1–25 outlines the most detail describing the reforms of Josiah, which are similar to those Hezekiah implemented after his father Ahaz had decimated the land of Judah with idolatry.

Read 2 Kings 23:1-25. *Take a highlighter and mark all these words in your Bible: bring, brought out, deposed, broke down, removed, burned, and pulled down.*

Referencing those words in the verses, fill in the blanks below—King Josiah . . .

Bring/brought out _____

Deposed _____

Broke down _____

Removed _____

Burned _____

Pulled down _____

Oh, that we would be this enthusiastic in identifying and tearing down our own idols. I know I have said this several times throughout the study, but can I repeat it? Idolatry is an abomination to God. Or, as we learned, God is disgusted by our idolatry; He loathes and hates it! I hope you can hear my passion to communicate earnestly to you that this is the very thing that keeps us from faithful living, not to mention leaving a lasting godly influence. If anything will be our undoing, it will be idolatry. The narratives of the kings have given us proof over and over again.

Will we soften our hearts and listen to God's warnings? Judah and Israel had God's messengers, the prophets. We have an entire book, the Bible, and the Holy Spirit who can help us overcome any stronghold that would keep God from being in the center of our hearts.

FIELDNOTES

As we close today, look below at the words we used to describe Josiah's reforms. Take a few minutes and ask God to show you if you need to do any of the same.

- Bring out (bring to light any sin in our heart)

- Depose (anyone in our life who influences us away from God)

- Remove (anything that tempts us away from God)

- Burn (not literally, but rid our life of any books, music, habits that lead us away from God)

- Pull down (any attitudes or thoughts that exalt themselves against God, e.g., bitterness, resentment, anger, etc. [see Eph. 4:29]).

Read Ephesians 4:22–24. *What does God call us to put on?*

What does He promise in 2 Corinthians 5:17?

Close today with a prayer of gratitude for God's mercy and grace.

THE LOST WORD

Just as Hezekiah had to clean up a great big mess in Judah, Josiah follows his ancestor Hezekiah's example by repairing and restoring the temple. The crowning event is reinstituting the Passover celebration. But before the Passover occurs, something happens when the temple is repaired that causes King Josiah great anguish. Something of great value was found—the book of the Law.

The Moody Bible Commentary explains the event:

> No explanation was given as to why this book (actually a scroll) was absent and where it might have been hidden or misplaced. Deuteronomy 31:24–26 states specifically that the law was to be placed next to the ark of the covenant. In addition, the king was to have access to this law on a regular basis so that he would know God's will. (cf. Dt. 17:14–20).[13]

SURVEY

Read 2 Kings 22:8–13.

After reading the details of the account, list any observations about this event.

What did Josiah do when he heard the words of the book of the Law?

Why do you think he was so moved by Hilkiah, the high priest, and what he found?

What does Josiah instruct Hilkiah to do in verse 13?

What do Hilkiah and the other three representatives go and find to authenticate this book of the Law in verse 14?

God chose the prophetess Huldah to deliver a message to Josiah. Other well-known prophets at the time included Jeremiah, Zephaniah, and Ezekiel. The high priest, along with three of the king's representatives—Achbor, Shaphan, and Asiah—went to consult with the Huldah the prophetess. She is the only female prophet in the entire list of prophets in the Old Testament besides Deborah in the book of Judges. It's interesting to note that God chose Huldah to deliver a message to Josiah "when other better-known male prophets such as Jeremiah, Zephaniah, and perhaps even Ezekiel, were also active at this time."[14] We don't know the reason, only that God chose Huldah to deliver the message.

"Another opinion. . . is that they had chosen a female prophet purposely, because 'women are merciful,' and they needed all the mercy and pleading before God that they could muster."[15]

Huldah wouldn't have been a true prophet if she wasn't obedient to the Lord in her words to the king. She didn't spare him the truth of the harsh message God delivered through her.

Read the account in 2 Kings 22:14–20. *List the events that were to take place in Judah.*

When does Huldah prophesy the events will occur?

What does God say about Josiah?

This particular part in the narrative gives proof of how God feels about His Word. Josiah was in deep anguish thinking he had missed an essential part of God's request that His people know and understand the law as given to Moses and to be handed down generation to generation.

Write out the rest of the sentence in verse 13: "For great is the wrath . . . "

What does Josiah note about God in this verse?

What does this verse say about Judah?

The main reason that Judah had gone astray was that they'd forgotten God's words to them. They failed to understand who Jehovah God was. They neglected His commandments and created their own truth according to the nations around them.

Does that sound at all familiar today? We live in a world that continues to ignore God, and we see the consequences of evil abound. It feels as though darkness has escalated in the past few years to unbelievable heights. God's Word is what will keep us anchored. It is the foundation that holds up our seven pillars of faithful living for lasting influence.

FIELDNOTES

When I was a teenager, I loved to read autobiographies. Some of the books that impacted me the most were books about persecuted Christians in the former Soviet Union. Since my mother's family was from Ukraine, I was drawn to stories of faith from that part of the world. The thread woven throughout all the stories was how God's Word sustained each person. Some of them only had scraps of pages of the Bible, and others had what they had memorized. This was their spiritual food when they were starved, beaten, tortured, and isolated and kept their spirits alive.

God's Word became more precious to me after I read their stories. My grandparents also underscored how grateful they were to have the freedom to have a Bible, as Bibles were scarce before my grandparents emigrated to the United States. I wish I could say that God's Word has always been important to me. There have been seasons of hurt and pain when I wasn't sure I could believe what I read. But in God's mercy, He drew me back to His Word as I confessed my fears and doubts. Now, after seeing God's faithfulness over and over again, I am passionate about others experiencing His Word.

Can you recall the first time you opened God's Word? What did it feel like?

What is one verse that has been an anchor for you?

WORSHIP OF THE WORD

Our last day of our last king has arrived. Josiah stands before his people and declares that they need to make a covenant after he publicly reads the book of the Law.

Read 2 Kings 23:1–3.

Describe the picture you might imagine if you were there. If you were a news reporter, how would you report this story?

What might your heart be feeling if you were standing in the crowd—

> *"all the inhabitants of Jerusalem and the priests and the prophets, all the people, both small and great" (v. 2)?*

Name the principles of the covenant that Josiah encouraged.

How can we follow suit? What does it look like for us to:

Walk after the Lord . . .

Keep His commandments and His statutes with all our heart and our soul . . .

After reading the Word and making the covenant, Josiah assigned the priests to specific tasks (2 Kings 23:4–20).

We created a list earlier this week; go back and review the list. How do you think the reading of God's Word impacted what the king decided to do?

EXCAVATE

When God's Word is central in our lives, it should motivate us to remove anything that would keep us from following Him with our whole hearts.

Think about the last time you read God's Word. Did it motivate you to take any action? What did you do?

Dear one, my prayer is for you to fall in love with God's Word so that it will help motivate you to faithful living permanently.

How can we take steps to make sure the Word of God stays central in our life?

Keeping the Word in the center of our life doesn't just happen. We have to be intentional about it. I used to think it was the quantity of Scripture I consumed that was important. It's not! It is whether I decide to feed myself daily and, in turn, how it helps me to live faithfully before God. But it doesn't happen if I don't have a plan of some sort.

Can I be tough for a moment? We really don't have any excuses. There are tools and resources and plans galore to help us get into the Word daily.

Do you have a plan for keeping God's Word in the center of your life? What does it look like?

What can you do this week to be intentional about soaking in God's Word?

FIELDNOTES

As we close out this week, I want us to look at one more part of Josiah's story. After Josiah cleaned up everything and swept idolatry from the land, it still wasn't enough to turn away God's judgment. Not because of Josiah, but because of the history of idolatry and wickedness in Judah.

> Before him there was no king like him, who turned to the LORD with all his heart and with all his soul and with all his might, according to all the Law of Moses, nor did any like him arise after him. Still, the LORD did not turn from the burning of his great wrath, by which his anger was kindled against Judah, because of all the provocations with which Manasseh had provoked him. And the LORD said, "I will remove Judah also out of my sight, as I have removed Israel, and I will cast off this city that I have chosen, Jerusalem, and the house of which I said, My name shall be there." (2 Kings 23:25–27).

You might be tempted to think, what's the point of being faithful if it doesn't change the future? I want to be very clear here. Faithful living doesn't mean we are responsible for the future. We don't have control over others or, for that matter, the outcome of events. God calls us to be faithful and follow Him in obedience. Whether or not God chooses to deliver us out of our circumstances or turn the tide of culture, we have to trust that He is sovereign, and He aligns His plans for His purposes. We have read several times in our study of how God allowed certain events to occur. This happened not to confuse or frustrate those involved, but rather to accomplish His purposes.

I started this study with the phrase "your faithfulness matters" and more importantly, faithfulness matters to God. We live in a rapidly deteriorating culture, one that is much like the nation of Judah when they forgot God. God has a purpose in everything He does, and even with the disheartening climate of our world, our faithfulness matters to God because we are a part of a bigger picture.

Recently, we had three of our grandchildren with us for what we call Camp Cavanaugh. I naively bought a 1,000-piece puzzle to put together, hoping it would entertain them and keep them busy. I didn't anticipate their finishing. As I worked with the youngest, who is seven, I marveled at her skill of finding the right piece in what was making me cross-eyed. By the time their five-day visit ended, the puzzle was finished. I found out their strategy: they didn't try to overthink it. They took it section by section, working on the pictures within the bigger picture and what it might look like. So, they started small, finding the pieces that made up the people in the beach scene, the sky with the birds, and the lighthouse until the whole picture became clear.

In the same way, that's what God asks of us. He doesn't expect us to see the big picture just yet. He asks us to be faithful to complete our section within the picture and let Him take care of the rest.

As we close this week, ask yourself: is there anything I am overthinking and feeling like my faithfulness doesn't seem to matter?

Write a prayer expressing how you have seen God's faithfulness in your life and how you might see a glimpse of the bigger picture.

PRAYER

Dear God . . .

Teshuvah and the Practice of Repentance

The Jewish people call the practice of repentance *Teshuvah*.

> *Teshuva*—returning—is the name Judaism gives to this process of retrieving our sense of direction. Repentance is the ultimate form of return. After turning our gaze away from God and straying from the straight path, we can still find our way back. And it is as simple as taking just one step in a new direction. For turning in a new direction, by as little as one degree, will lead us over time to a wholly different destination.
>
> Doing *Teshuva*, turning away from sin, is all about choosing God over idolatry, truth over deception (including self-deception).[16]

Here is a simple way to practice repentance using the word "repent" as an acrostic.

R - Recognize and name your sin, don't delay

E - Expect God to hear your confession

P - Practice giving and receiving forgiveness

E - Embrace the truth of Galatians 6:1

N - Nail your sin to the cross

T - Turn away and do the right thing marked by your actions

Manasseh did this; he experienced *Teshuva* by turning completely away from his sin and moving in another direction. In the last years of his life, "he took away the foreign gods and the idol from the house of the LORD, and all the altars that he had built on the mountain of the house of the LORD and in Jerusalem, and he threw them outside of the city. He also restored the altar of the LORD" (2 Chron. 33:15–16). His actions marked his repentance. He changed his mind about his sin and turned back to the Lord.

When we practice complete repentance, the fruit is evident in our behavior. Our belief system of independence, pride, and entitlement shifts to bringing us to a state of humility before God. We then desire to do everything possible to turn back to God and make sure our actions mark our newness to make things right with God and others.

My Live Bold
Legacy Covenant

REMEMBERING HERITAGE

"And the king stood by the pillar and made a covenant before the
LORD, to walk after the LORD and to keep his commandments and his
testimonies and his statutes with all his heart and all his soul, to perform
the words of this covenant that were written in this book.
And all the people joined in the covenant."
2 KINGS 23:3

Can you believe it? We have arrived at the end of our biblical archaeological dig
into the lives of the eight godly kings of Judah. Together we've faithfully surveyed,
excavated, and made fieldnotes on each of the kings. We've extracted an enormous
amount of information, both historically and theologically from the Scriptures.
Now we'll bring our biblical archaeological dig to a close and summarize what
we've learned. Once archaeologists have finished a dig, they analyze all the artifacts and information they've obtained to "report on their research and curate the
collection."[1] It's time to hang up our tools and make some final observations.

This week will look a little different. Instead of having five days of in-depth study,
you will have sections to work through at your own pace. I'd like to encourage you

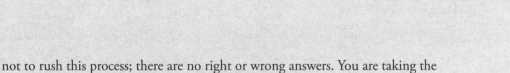

not to rush this process; there are no right or wrong answers. You are taking the theological data and artifacts you've collected along the way to summarize for your spiritual growth. This is for *you*.

Let me encourage you to take the time required to bring application so that you can create your personal legacy covenant with the seven pillars for faithful living and lasting influence. This may take more than a week, but make a goal to wrap up your summary within two weeks.

When you are finished curating your takeaways, you will transfer them into your own personal My Live Bold Legacy Covenant. The completed covenant follows Week Eight, which you can refer to as a reminder so that you can continue in the steps to live victoriously and faithfully.

In my experience, working through a Bible study is nearly always rewarding. However, it's now up to me before I place the finished study on my shelf to inspire transformation from the truth I've learned.

Before we review the data we've collected in our Fieldnotes, I want to discuss two concepts. The first is introducing our seventh and final pillar of faithful living for lasting influence—***Remembering Heritage***. Part of leaving a lasting legacy is remembering the past, not to dwell on our hurts or pain but rather to remember the markers along the way where we have seen God's faithfulness. These markers can give us courage in the next challenging season and help us instill courage in the next generation.

Remembering is a pattern we see throughout the Old Testament, and Psalm 143:5 reminds us, "I remember the days of old; I meditate on all that you have done; I ponder the work of your hands."

What do the following verses tell us about the significance of remembering?

Exodus 13:3

Deuteronomy 8:2

Deuteronomy 32:7

Psalm 77:11

Psalm 105:5

Isaiah 46:9

What did you learn about God in these verses?

An exercise I try to practice each December as I am praying about my word for the coming year is to review the past twelve months and mark the faithfulness of God, remembering His goodness and how He helped me remain faithful to Him. This has empowered my faith in two ways. First, it creates a sense of gratitude, realizing how God's character shows me kindness, faithfulness, mercy, and goodness.

The second is it gives me a record when I have spiritual amnesia in a challenging season. I can look back and remember that if God was faithful to me last year, five years ago, or ten years ago, He will be faithful to me in my present challenge. I also keep track of it in a visual journal, and someday when I graduate to heaven, I hope the journal will be a source of inspiration for my children and grandchildren.

Think back over the past year. Can you remember and testify of God's recent faithfulness in your life? List the ways He has shown His faithfulness.

Next, I'll give you a bit of an intro on covenant. We are going to look at what God says about the word "covenant" in a few Scriptures, and the promises He gives when we keep covenant with Him. As we reflect on the following verses and then create a covenant, I want you to see how important covenant keeping is to God.

What does God promise in the following verses if we keep covenant with God to follow Him in obedience?

Psalm 25:14

Psalm 103:17–18

Psalm 105:8

Deuteronomy 7:9

Write out a summary of your findings.

In a Bible dictionary or commentary, look up the definition of "covenant."
(Note: A great online resource is www.blueletterbible.org, which gives you many options for researching a word in the Bible.)

What did you discover about the meaning of "covenant"?

From what you learned over the past seven weeks, has your understanding of the significance of following God in obedience changed? If so, share your thoughts.

As we think about all that we've learned, keep in mind what Andrew Murray says about entering into covenant with God:

> Wholeheartedness is the secret of entering the Covenant, and God being found of us in it. Wholeheartedness is the secret of joy in religion—a full entrance into all the blessedness the Covenant brings. God rejoices over His people to do them good.[2]

As you think about ways to strengthen your faith, this exercise will give you a tool to help you intentionally continue in faithful living.

Let's get started!

Step One: This section will review our Fieldnotes for each week. We'll distill these into one or two transformational truths that apply in this season of your life. You can use the questions in the Fieldnotes Truth category in the chart to inspire your reflection as you fill in the boxes.

Step Two: List a Scripture in the Sealing Scripture box that helps to seal the truth you've discovered. You can choose a verse from this Bible study or another one that God has given you for this truth. (You will also transfer the verse to your My Live Bold Legacy Covenant.)

WEEK	FIELDNOTES TRUTH	SEALING SCRIPTURE
WEEK ONE: CHRONICLES OF THE KINGS OVERVIEW	Who in your life is a voice of truth?	
WEEK TWO: REVIVING OBEDIENCE King Asa and King Jehoshaphat	What is something specific you can do to remove any "high places" in your life?	
WEEK THREE: RENEWING TRUST King Joash	What are some steps we can take to make sure we aren't living a secondhand faith? How can I be sure to love the Lord my God with all of my heart, my soul, and my mind?	
WEEK FOUR: RECEIVING WISDOM King Amaziah	What is the best way for me to listen to God?	
WEEK FIVE: RELENTLESS FAITH King Uzziah and King Jotham	What can I do to strengthen my armor? How can I protect my heart from pride?	

WEEK	FIELDNOTES TRUTH	SEALING SCRIPTURE
WEEK SIX: **REFORMING PRAYER** King Hezekiah	How can you build worship and prayer into your life in a more powerful way?	
WEEK SEVEN: **REBUILDING WORSHIP** King Josiah	How does remembering God's Word impact your influence?	
WEEK EIGHT: **REMEMBERING HERITAGE** My Live Bold Legacy Covenant	What are some significant spiritual markers in your life? The covenant is a tangible reminder of intentionally seeking to follow God with our whole hearts. How can you practice keeping covenant with God to live faithfully?	

Yay! You did it! I have one last summary task before we close the study. Looking over your Fieldnotes and Scripture from the previous chart, choose the three most significant truths you've learned throughout *The Godly Kings of Judah*. Write briefly what God taught you, the sealing Scripture, and your next steps or plan of action to apply what you've learned.

TRUTH #1
Summary of what God taught me:

Scripture:

What I will do:

TRUTH #2
Summary of what God taught me:

Scripture:

What I will do:

TRUTH #3
Summary of what God taught me:

Scripture:

What I will do:

Your very last step will be to transfer your summary from the chart to personalize your My Live Bold Legacy Covenant on the following page. You can remove the page and place it somewhere where you can be reminded of your intentions to follow God in obedience.

This covenant includes the seven pillars and your commitment to live faithfully and leave a lasting influence.

Final Thoughts and Blessing

We've come to the end of our study, and as I've said many times over the past weeks—I am so incredibly proud of you! Can you see me smiling and dancing with joy? You have succeeded in becoming a biblical archeologist and brilliantly used your tools to dig out transforming truth. Thank you for walking this journey, *The Godly Kings of Judah: Faithful Living for Lasting Influence.*

I wish I could invite each of you to my home for some decadent cake and coffee or tea. I imagine us sitting in my living room with our Bibles on our laps revealing the treasures we've found in *The Godly Kings of Judah.* Next, I would sit down at the piano and ask you to join me before we part in singing the worship song, *The Blessing.*[3] The song summarizes my love and heart for each of you. When you close the last page of the Bible study, I hope you'll find that song on the internet and listen closely to the words which come from Scripture. My prayer is that God will continue to teach you His truth so that you can leave a wholehearted legacy of faith for the generations to follow.

> "The Lord bless you and keep you; the Lord make his face
> to shine upon you and be gracious to you; the Lord lift up
> his countenance upon you and give you peace."
>
> **Numbers 6:24–26**

My Live Bold Legacy Covenant

Dear God,

This is my Live Bold Legacy Covenant, and with the Holy Spirit's help, I choose to be intentional about these seven pillars, so that I may live faithfully for You and build a lasting godly influence.

REVIVING OBEDIENCE

My desire is to . . .

Sealing Scripture:

RENEWING TRUST

My desire is to . . .

Sealing Scripture:

RECEIVING WISDOM

My desire is to . . .

Sealing Scripture:

RELENTLESS FAITH

My desire is to . . .

Sealing Scripture:

REFORMING PRAYER

My desire is to . . .

Sealing Scripture:

REBUILDING WORSHIP

My desire is to . . .

Sealing Scripture:

REMEMBERING HERITAGE

My desire is to . . .

Sealing Scripture:

YOUR NAME:

DATE:

7 Pillars for Faithful Living and Lasting Influence

We will all leave a legacy. We have a choice of what we will pass on to the generations. Remembering the spiritual markers in our lives help us to move forward.

Reviving Obedience (Week Two)

Obedience unlocks the door to faithful living and comes from cultivating ongoing revival in our hearts.

Renewing Trust (Week Three)

Renewing our trust in Jesus is not just a one-time event. In order to follow Christ faithfully, we need to renew our trust often, even daily.

Receiving Wisdom (Week Four)

Listening to godly voices is important in developing wisdom and discernment.

Relentless Faith (Week Five)

Part of living faithfully is having the courage to persevere and be relentless through the triumphs and trials of life.

Reforming Prayer (Week Six)

Without prayer, faithful living is hard to do on our own. Embracing a life of prayer reforms our attitudes and behaviors.

Rebuilding Worship (Week Seven)

Worship keeps our hearts soft. Examining our altars of worship are important to faithfully follow God with a whole heart.

Remembering Heritage (Week Eight)

Recalling God's faithfulness helps us to continue on the path of righteous living and gives us courage to leave a godly legacy for the generations to come.

"And I am sure of this, that he who began a good work in you
will bring it to completion at the day of Jesus Christ."

Philippians 1:6

KINGS GENEALOGY TIMELINE WITH PROPHETS[1]

Kings of Israel—Northern Kingdom

Name of King	Date of Reign (year) some coregent	Relation to Predecessor	Reign	1-2 Kings, 1-2 Chronicles Reference	Prophet
Jeroboam I	931–910 (22)	servant	bad	1Kg 11:26–14:20; 2Ch 9:29–13:22	
Nadab	910–909 (2)	son	bad	1Kg 15:25–28	
Baasha	909–886 (24)	none	bad	1Kg 15:27–16:7; 2Ch 16:1–6	
Elah	886–885 (2)	son	bad	1Kg 16:6–14	
Zimri	885 (7 days)	horse captain	bad	1Kg 16:9–20	
Omri	885–874 (12)	army captain	bad	1Kg 16:15–28	
Ahab	874–853 (22)	son	bad	1Kg 16:28–22:40; 2Ch 18:1–34	Elijah, Micaiah
Ahaziah	853–852 (2)	son	bad	1Kg 22:40–2Kg 1:18; 2Ch 20:35–37	Elijah
Jehoram/Joram	852–841 (12)	brother	bad	2Kg 3:1–9:25; 2Ch 22:5–7	Elijah
Jehu	841–814 (28)	none	bad	2Kg 9:1–10:36; 2Ch 22:7–12	Elisha
Jehoahaz	814–798 (17)	son	bad	2Kg 13:1–9	Elisha
Jehoash/Joash	798–782 (16)	son	bad	2Kg 13:10–14:16; 2Ch 25:17–24	Elisha
Jeroboam II	793–753 (41)	son	bad	2Kg 14:23–29	Hosea, Amos, Jonah
Zechariah	753–752 (6 months)	son	bad	2Kg 14:29–15:12	
Shallum	752 (1 month)	none	bad	2Kg 15:10–15	
Menahem	752–742 (10)	none	bad	2Kg 15:14–22	
Pekahiah	742–740 (2)	son	bad	2Kg 15:22–26	
Pekah	752–731 (20)	army captain	bad	2Kg 15:27–31; 2Ch 28:5–8	
Hoshea	731–722/21 (9)	none	bad	2Kg 15:30–17:6	

Kings of Judah—Southern Kingdom

Name of King	Date of Reign (year) some coregent	Relation to Predecessor	Reign	1-2 Kings, 1-2 Chronicles Reference	Prophet
Rehoboam	931–913 (17)	Solomon's son	bad	1Kg 11:42–41:31; 2Ch 9:31–12:16	
Abijam/Abijah	913–911 (3)	son	bad	1Kg 14:31–15:8; 2Ch 13:1–22	
Asa	911–870 (41)	son	good	1Kg 15:8–24; 2Ch 14:1–16:14	
Jehoshaphat	873–848 (25)	son	good	1Kg 22:41–50; 2Ch 17:1–20:37	
Jehoram/Joram	848–841 (8)	son	bad	2Kg 8:16–24; 2Ch 21:1–20	
Ahaziah	841 (1)	son	bad	2Kg 8:24–9:29; 2Ch 22:1–9	
Athaliah (Queen)	841–835 (6)	mother	bad	2Kg 11:1–20; 2Ch 22:1–23:21	
Joash/Jehoash	835–796 (40)	grandson	good	2Kg 11:1–12:21; 2Ch 22:10–24:27	
Amaziah	796–767 (29)	son	good	2Kg 14:1–20; 2Ch 25:1–28	
Azariah/Uzziah	792–740 (52)	son	good	2Kg 15:1–7; 2Ch 26:1–23	Isaiah, Hosea, Amos
Jotham	750–732 (16)	son	good	2Kg 15:32–38; 2Ch 27:1–9	Isaiah, Hosea, Micah
Ahaz	735–716 (16)	son	bad	2Kg 16:1–20; 2Ch 28:1–27	Isaiah, Hosea, Micah
Hezekiah	716/15–687 (29)	son	good	2Kg 18:1–20:21; 2Ch 29:1–32:33	Isaiah, Hosea, Micah
Manasseh	697–643 (55)	son	bad	2Kg 21:1–18; 2Ch 33:1–29	
Amon	643–641 (2)	son	bad	2Kg 21:19–26; 2Ch 33:21–25	
Josiah	641–609 (31)	son	good	2Kg 22:1–23:30; 2Ch 34:1–35:27	Jeremiah, Zephaniah
Jehoahaz	609 (3 months)	son	bad	2Kg 23:31–33; 2Ch 36:1–4	Jeremiah
Jehoiakim	609–598 (11)	brother	bad	2Kg 23:34–24:5; 2Ch 36:5–7	Jeremiah, Habakkuk
Jehoiachin	589–597 (3 months)	son	bad	2Kg 24:6–16; 2Ch 36:8–10	Jeremiah
Zedekiah	597–586 (11)	son	bad	2Kg 24:17–25:30; 2Ch 36:11–21	Jeremiah

MAP OF THE NORTHERN AND SOUTHERN KINGDOMS[1]

931 BC to 586 BC

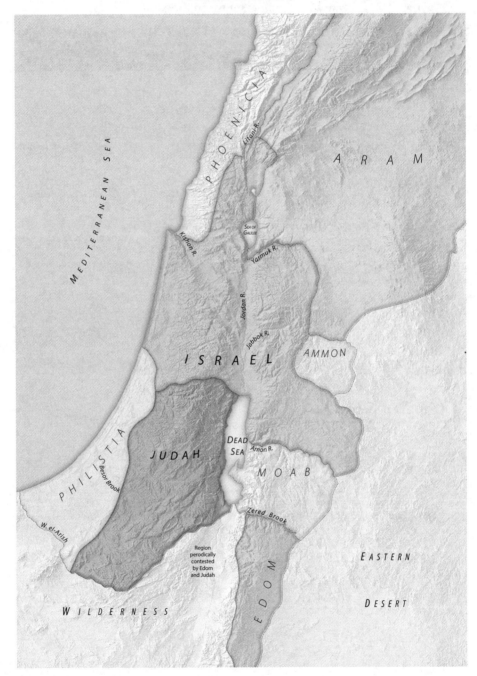

MEDITERRANEAN SEA

PHOENICIA

ARAM

Litani R.

Kishon R.

SEA OF GALILEE

Yarmuk R.

Jordan R.

Jabbok R.

ISRAEL

AMMON

PHILISTIA

Besor Brook

JUDAH

DEAD SEA

Arnon R.

MOAB

W. el-Arish

Zered Brook

Region perodically contested by Edom and Judah

EDOM

EASTERN

DESERT

WILDERNESS

LEADER'S GUIDE

You are a leader! Yes, YOU! Now don't look around behind you to see if I am talking about someone else; I am speaking to you! Maybe right now, you don't feel qualified to lead a small group of women through a Bible study, but it's no accident you are here. Whether you volunteered in a moment of weakness or are a seasoned leader, I believe God will use *you* to influence the women in your group to hunger and thirst after Jesus.

You might not see yourself as a leader, so let's define it differently. A leader is an influencer. If you are a mom, helper in a classroom, teacher, boss, Sunday school teacher, youth mentor, or neighborhood-event planner, you are qualified to lead!

You are an *influencer*. The *Merriam-Webster Dictionary* defines an influencer as "one who exerts influence: a person who inspires or guides the actions of others."[1] That's you! Your role as a leader of this Bible study is to inspire and guide the women with the help of the Holy Spirit to help them fall more in love with Jesus.

I've found in my experience leading women that the women who come to your group need just two things:

1. To be loved

2. To be prayed for

That's it! If you can love the women in your group and pray for them, you will be a great leader. The rest of the skills you need are all accessible and can be learned; all you need to do is ask for help. I have to admit that I learned this the hard way. In my early years of being a rookie leader, my focus in leading women was all about the task. I was checking off the boxes, getting the answers, and finishing the discussion. I wanted them to get 'er done! I did pray for the women in my group but more as a "group prayer" instead of genuinely being interested in their lives. As God developed my infant leadership skills and I observed other women influencers, I came to understand what it means to shepherd and care for the women in my group.

Here are a few tips to help you get started, and then I will outline each chapter and what I suggest you can work through in your discussion time centered around a theme.

As a small group leader of a Bible study, imagine yourself as a coach. As a coach, you help the women process what they learn by asking questions through discussion. You don't have to do all the talking; in fact, if you do, then you aren't really leading; you are just talking. I've found these five steps to be helpful.

1. Be authentic—be who God created you to be and be transparent. Take a step of faith to lead the discussion by being vulnerable with a personal story, struggle, or what you are working through. Trust me; if you go first once in a while, people will open up!

2. You don't have to have all the answers. Look to others in the group for help. You might say, "What do you think about Susan's question?" And let the group talk. If no one knows the answer, be willing to do some homework before the following week.

3. Ask questions and wait for others to answer. Don't feel like you have to fill a silent gap. Give it more than five seconds.

4. Listen, and listen intently. Don't think of what question you must ask next. Pause and reflect on what the person is saying. Often another question might come from what someone is sharing that will direct the group. Listen to the Holy Spirit, and trust that He will lead you to lead the women.

5. Be prepared! It's hard to be authentic, listen, and ask good questions if you haven't taken the time to prepare. Spend time during the week as you are working through the study to pray for the women in your group and any part of the study that you believe might be an essential focus based on the needs of your group.

The guide for each week is just that—a guide of a suggested format of how to lead your discussion time. Don't stress if you don't get through every question! Sometimes the richest discussions come from focusing on one truth. Let the Holy Spirit be your guide. Remember, the goal is meaningful conversation pointing the women back to Jesus.

Are you ready? I am cheering you on from the sidelines and can't wait for God to meet you and your women in *The Godly Kings of Judah*.

Start Here

WEEK ONE: CHRONICLES OF THE KINGS OVERVIEW

As you gather in your group for the first week, spend some time getting to know one another before you dive into the week's discussion. A few suggested questions might be:

1. What are your expectations for joining this Bible study?
2. Define faithfulness; what does it mean to you?
3. Have you read the section, *How to make the most of this study?* Any questions?

However you begin, make sure you always start with prayer inviting the Holy Spirit into your group time.

Theme: Historical overview and events leading up to the divided kingdom

DAY ONE: What did you discover in looking at the big picture of the kings?

DAY TWO: What do you think Solomon could have done differently to stay on the path of faithfulness as his father King David did? What can we do to make sure we don't follow Solomon's example?

DAY THREE: Fieldnotes Question—What happens when you follow your own path?

DAY FOUR: What did you learn about the role of the prophets in Judah? Do you have a voice of wisdom in your life to help hold you accountable?

DAY FIVE: Share one of the three new facts you learned about the history of the kings of Judah that you didn't know before.

WEEK TWO: KING ASA AND KING JEHOSHAPHAT—REVIVING OBEDIENCE

Theme: Tearing down family high places and obedience

DAY ONE: What are some significant characteristics about King Asa in your observations from the reading?

Fieldnotes—Discuss how do family members influence our faith?

DAY TWO: Fieldnotes—Share one of your high places, Scripture, and plan (from the chart) to overcome and tear down a high place in your life.

DAY THREE: How can we gain the courage to walk in obedience toward revival?

DAY FOUR: Contrast King Asa and his son Jehoshaphat from reading Scripture. What are the similarities and differences?

What steps can we take to break a generational sin by the example of King Asa and King Jehoshaphat?

DAY FIVE: What are ways Christians make alliances that are unhealthy?

WEEK THREE: KING JOASH—RENEWING TRUST

Theme: Being intentional about developing your relationship and trust in Jesus, not living a secondhand faith

DAY ONE: Discuss the key players surrounding King Joash from your notes in 2 Kings 11 and 12.

DAY TWO: Fieldnotes—What does a wise woman do to build her house? Contrast what Athaliah did in tearing down her family.

DAY THREE: Discuss the influence of Jehoiada and Jehosheba on King Joash from your study.

Who needs your influence and encouragement?

DAY FOUR: From your study, what did the relationship look like between Jehoiada and Joash?

DAY FIVE: With Jehoiada out of the picture, what happened? Why did Joash turn? How can we prevent having a secondhand faith? What does becoming a critical thinker mean?

WEEK FOUR: KING AMAZIAH—RECEIVING WISDOM

Theme—Importance of listening to God to receive wisdom

DAY ONE: Discuss what you think about the queen mother's influence from your reading.

DAY TWO: What is the power of a mother's influence?

DAY THREE: In what situation did Abigail find herself encountering King David? Have you ever felt stuck in circumstances that are beyond your control?

Fieldnotes—What lie keeps you from believing God in your circumstance? What Scripture do you need to preach to yourself?

DAY FOUR: Have you ever been faced with a listening crisis? What happened?

What did Amaziah miss in not listening to God? What was his response in 2 Chronicles 25:16?

DAY FIVE: What did you write down in the Fieldnotes regarding the next godly step to listen to God?

If you have time, you may want to discuss the Artifacts: Digging Deeper section and the influence of the queen mothers.

WEEK FIVE: KING UZZIAH AND KING JOTHAM—RELENTLESS FAITH

Theme—Fighting the battle—know your enemy, prepare, surround yourself with the right voices

DAY ONE: What does it look like to have relentless faith? Is there a story in your life or someone you know that has experienced relentless faith? What is your temptation when your heart wants to give up?

DAY TWO: How can we surround ourselves with the right voices? What was King Uzziah's example? What are some of the consequences of not listening, according to Proverbs?

DAY THREE: How well do you know your enemy, according to the assessment?

Read 1 Peter 5:6–7. How can we become more aware of the enemy's tactics? Did you find a theme of Satan's tactics in the verses listed in the Excavate section?

DAY FOUR: What did you learn about Uzziah entering the inner sanctum of the temple? Summarize what God says about pride in the Survey section.

What did you learn about the opposite of pride—humility? How does knowing our enemy help us defeat pride?

DAY FIVE: How was Jotham's reign different from his father, Uzziah? Do you think he played it safe? Why or why not?

WEEK SIX: KING HEZEKIAH—REFORMING PRAYER

Theme—Prayer leads to reform and victory

DAY ONE: What is your observation about King Hezekiah's life from your reading? What is your one truth that stands out above the rest?

DAY TWO: What were the differences between Ahaz and his son Hezekiah? How do you think Ahaz's destructive ways impacted Hezekiah?

In the Excavate section, what do the verses listed tell you about God's promises to us? Is there a place in your heart you've shut the door to prayer and worship? What is the step you are willing to take?

DAY THREE: Describe Hezekiah's prayer. Have you ever been in a similar situation? What did you do?

DAY FOUR: What are some practical ways we can practice Hezekiah's example of prayer?

DAY FIVE: What are your hopes and dreams for future generations?

You may want to close your group in a time of prayer, practicing some of the suggestions that were mentioned in the group.

WEEK SEVEN: KING JOSIAH—REBUILDING WORSHIP

Theme—Repentance and rebuilding worship

DAY ONE: How can knowing God's Word help us keep from practicing idolatry? How are half-truths permeating our culture today?

DAY TWO: What does Manasseh do that causes God to have compassion on him? How does God show mercy to us? Is there a Bible verse that we read this week that is meaningful to you in remembering God's compassion?

DAY THREE: What does genuine repentance look like? Why is it so important to God?

DAY FOUR: Look back at your Fieldnotes and share any reforms God is asking you to make.

What does Ephesians 4:22–24 say we are to put on?

DAY FIVE: How did Josiah's response to finding the book of the Law impact you?

Fieldnotes—When is the first time you opened God's Word? What is one verse that has been an anchor for you?

If you have time, you might want to discuss the Artifacts: Digging Deeper section on the topic of repentance.

WEEK EIGHT: MY LIVE BOLD LEGACY COVENANT— REMEMBERING HERITAGE

Theme—Intentional plan to live faithfully

Discuss what it means to remember God's faithfulness. Encourage each of the women to share a time they can remember God's faithfulness. After each woman has shared, take time to express prayers of gratitude.

Encourage your group to keep working on their Live Bold Legacy Covenant if they couldn't complete it. In closing, have them choose one of the seven pillars and share what they've reflected and written as their desire and sealing Scripture.

ACKNOWLEDGMENTS

To all my sister prayer warriors and friends who prayed me to the finish line of *The Godly Kings of Judah*—my Aunt Trudy, cousin Andrea, lifelong friend Cheryl, sister Heidi, mentor and friend Heidi M., Edie, Carol, coach and friend, Janet, Carole, Debbie, Erica, Athena, Cynthia, and a host of other women too numerous to mention! You gave me the courage to keep writing and words of strength to keep looking up in a difficult season. Thank you for your texts, cards, emails, social media posts, and special gifts of remembrance, including dark chocolate!

To my family, who cheered me on from the sidelines and who continues to believe in me pursuing God's gift of writing even when it means I can't be available for a season.

To Judy Dunagan—acquisition editor at Moody Publishers, and my dear friend— whose passionate pursuit of prayer and godly wisdom encourages me to press in deeper to Jesus.

To the women at Cedar Grove Church who encouraged me as a fledgling writer years ago as I tested the waters in writing and teaching Bible studies.

To Moody Publishers—Amanda Cleary Eastep, senior developmental editor, who I instantly connected with, for her patience working through the maze of edits, especially with all the names between the books of Kings and Chronicles. Ashley Torres and her brilliant marketing expertise and the rest of the publishing team. It is a great honor to be represented by an organization whose staff walks with biblical integrity and is prayerful about each project from start to finish. Thank you for believing in me and *The Godly Kings of Judah* Bible study.

To the one true King I love with my whole heart, King Jesus. From studying the godly kings, You've taught me more about Your unfathomable mercy—that living faithfully doesn't come from striving for perfection but rather in being still, listening, and trusting in obedience. May this study be an offering of thanksgiving and one that pleases You and gives You all the honor, praise, and glory.

NOTES

Introduction

1. *National Treasure*, directed by Jon Turteltaub (2004; Buena Vista, CA: Walt Disney Studios).

Week One: Chronicles of the Kings Overview

1. "OT325: Book Study: 1 & 2 Kings," Logos Mobile Education (Bellingham, WA: Lexham Press, 2016).

2. Kevin D. Zuber, "1 Chronicles," in *The Moody Bible Commentary*, Michael Rydelnik and Michael Vanlaningham, gen. eds. (Chicago: Moody, 2014), 554–55.

3. C. Knapp, *Kings of Judah* (Dubuque, IA: ECS Ministries, 1909, revised 2004), 19, 22.

4. Mark Leuchter and David Lamb, *The Historical Writings: Introducing Israel's Historical Literature* (Minneapolis: Fortress Press, 2016), 260.

5. Harry E. Shields, "2 Kings," in *The Moody Bible Commentary*, 480.

6. Leuchter and Lamb, *The Historical Writings*, 284.

7. "OT325: Book Study: 1 & 2 Kings," Logos Mobile Education.

8. "Regnal," *Merriam Webster's Collegiate Dictionary*, 11th ed., 2020.

9. David T. Lamb, *OT325: Book Study: 1 & 2 Kings* (Minneapolis: Fortress Press, 2016), 269.

10. "Strong's H4931—mismeret," (ESV), Blue Letter Bible, https://www .blueletterbible.org/lexicon/h4931/esv/wlc/0-1/.

11. Louis E. Newman, *Repentance: The Meaning and Practice of Teshuvah* (Woodstock, VT: Jewish Lights Publishing, 2010), 33.

12. Abraham Lincoln, House Divided Speech, June 16, 1868, Collected Works of Abraham Lincoln, http://www.abrahamlincolnonline.org/lincoln/speeches/ house.htm.

13. *NKJV Cultural Backgrounds Study Bible*, "Temples and Sacred Spaces" (Grand Rapids, MI: Zondervan, 2017), 751.

14. Ibid., 615.

15. "OT325: Book Study: 1 & 2 Kings," Logos Mobile Education.

16. Ibid.

17. Leuchter and Lamb, *The Historical Writings*, 272.

18. Zuber, "2 Chronicles," in *The Moody Bible Commentary*, 600.

Week Two: Reviving Obedience

1. "Asa," Strong's H609, Blue Letter Bible, https://www.blueletterbible.org/lexicon/h609/kjv/wlc/0-1.

2. "Jehoshaphat," Strong's H3092, Blue Letter Bible, https://www.blueletterbible.org/lexicon/h3092/esv/wlc/0-1.

3. Diane Severance, "When Revival Ran Epidemic," Christianity.com, https://www.christianity.com/church/church-history/timeline/1801-1900/when-revival-ran-epidemic-11630508.html.

4. Lowell K. Handy, "Bible Study and the Moody Bible Institute: From Dryer to Peterman," paper for Chicago Society of Bible and Research, April 24, 2010, Biographical Files, Moody Bible Institute, Chicago.

5. Jamie Janosz, *When Others Shuddered: Eight Women Who Refused to Give Up* (Chicago: Moody, 2014), 36–47.

6. James Strong, *A Concise Dictionary of the Words in the Greek Testament and the Hebrew Bible* (Peabody, MA: Hendrickson Publishing, 2009), 2388.

7. Cynthia Cavanaugh, *Live Unveiled: Freedom to Worship God, Love Others, and Tell Your Story* (Enumclaw, WA: Redemption Press, 2017), 72.

8. *Tombstone*, directed by George P. Cosmatos and Kevin Jarre (1993; Burbank, CA: Hollywood Pictures).

9. Kevin D. Zuber, "2 Chronicles," in *The Moody Bible Commentary*, Michael Rydelnik and Michael Vanlaningham, gen. eds. (Chicago: Moody, 2014), 614.

10. John D. Barry et al., eds., *The Lexham Bible Dictionary*, 2016, Digital Logos Bible Software.

11. Ibid.

12. Ibid.

Week Three: Renewing Trust

1. "Strong's H3101—yoas," (KJV), Blue Letter Bible, https://www.blueletterbible.org/lexicon/h3101/kjv/wlc/0-1.

2. https://www.history.com/shows/alone.

3. James Strong, *A Concise Dictionary of the Words in the Greek Testament and the Hebrew Bible* (Peabody, MA: Hendrickson Publishing, 2009), 5255.

4. Justin Dillehay and Ivan Mesa, "Bible Literacy Crisis!," *The Gospel Coalition*, January 14, 2020, https://www.thegospelcoalition.org/article/bible-literacy-crisis/.

5. "High Priest—Easton's Bible Dictionary," Blue Letter Bible, https://www.blueletterbible.org/search/dictionary/viewtopic.cfm?topic.

6. "Priest, High – International Standard Bible Encyclopaedia," Blue Letter Bible, https://www.blueletterbible.org/search/dictionary/viewtopic.cfm.

Week Four: Receiving Wisdom

1. "Strong's H558—amasya," (KJV), Blue Letter Bible, https://www.blueletterbible.org/lexicon/h558/kjv/wlc/0-1.

2. Becky Harling, *How to Listen So People Will Talk: Build Stronger Communications and Deeper Connection*. Bloomington, MN: Bethany House, 2017).

3. C. Knapp, *Kings of Judah* (Dubuque, IA: ECS Ministries, 1909, revised 2004), 87.

4. Niels-Erik A. Andreasen, "*The Role of the Queen Mother in Israelite Society*," *The Catholic Biblical Quarterly*, April 1983, vol. 45, no. 2 (April 1983), 191 Catholic Biblical Association, Stable URL: https://www.jstor.org/stable/43719002.

5. Rob Olason, The Vigil, https://blaineicelanders.com/2018/09/24/the-vigil-blaine-washington-u-s-a/.

6. Cynthia Cavanaugh, "Stay in Your Lane: Find Your Focus," *Nourish: Encouragement for Women in Leadership*, Moody Publishers Women, no. 12 (July 2021): 18.

7. Brian Bowen, "Mothers and Sons: Queen Mothers of Judah and the Religious Trends that Develop During Their Sons' Reign," (2021), Honors Program Projects, 120, 22, https://digitalcommons.olivet.edu/honr_proj/120.

Week Five: Relentless Faith

1. https://www.blueletterbible.org/lexicon/h5818/kjv/wlc/0-1.
2. "Strong's H3147—yotam," (KJV), Blue Letter Bible, https://www.blueletterbible.org/lexicon/h3147/kjv/wlc/0-1.
3. C. Knapp, *Kings of Judah* (Dubuque, IA: ECS Ministries, 1909, revised 2004), 95.
4. John D. Barry et al., eds., *The Lexham Bible Dictionary*, 2016, Digital Logos Bible Software.
5. Kevin D. Zuber, "2 Chronicles," in *The Moody Bible Commentary*, Michael Rydelnik and Michael Vanlaningham, gen. eds. (Chicago: Moody, 2014), 621.
6. Mark Bubeck, *Warfare Praying: Biblical Strategies for Overcoming the Adversary* (Chicago: Moody, 1984, 2016), 29.
7. Knapp, *Kings of Judah*, 104.
8. Zuber, "1 Chronicles," in *The Moody Bible Commentary*, 622.
9. Knapp, *Kings of Judah*, 100.
10. "Philistines—Easton's Bible Dictionary," Blue Letter Bible, https://www.blueletterbible.org/search/dictionary/viewtopic.cfm?topic=ET0002940.
11. "Arabians," *Smith's Bible Dictionary*, Blue Letter Bible, https://www.blueletterbible.org/search/dictionary/viewtopic.cfm?topic=BT0000354.
12. "Menuites," *Encyclopaedia Judaica,* 2008, The Gale Group, https://www.jewishvirtuallibrary.org/meunites.

Week Six: Reforming Prayer

1. "Strong's H2396—hizqiya," (KJV), Blue Letter Bible, https://www.blueletterbible.org/lexicon/h2396/kjv/wlc/0-1.
2. Kevin D. Zuber, "2 Chronicles," in *The Moody Bible Commentary*, Michael Rydelnik and Michael Vanlaningham, gen. eds. (Chicago: Moody, 2014), 623.
3. Lynn Austin, The Chronicles of the Kings: *Gods and Kings* (Bloomington: Bethany House, 2005).
4. Erica Belibtreu, "Grisly Record of Torture and Death," *Biblical Archaeology Society* 17, no. 1 (Jan/Feb 1991): https://faculty.uml.edu/ethan_spanier/teaching/documents/cp6.0assyriantorture.pdf.

5. John D. Barry et al., eds., *The Lexham Bible Dictionary*, 2016, Digital Logos Bible Software.

Week Seven: Rebuilding Worship

1. "Strong's H2977—yosiya," (KJV), Blue Letter Bible, https://www.blueletterbible .org/lexicon/h2977/kjv/wlc/0-1.

2. C. H. Spurgeon, "Pardon for the Greatest Guilt," No. 2378, https://www .spurgeongems.org/sermon/chs2378.pdf.

3. James Strong, *A Concise Dictionary of the Words in the Greek Testament and the Hebrew Bible* (Peabody, MA: Hendrickson Publishing, 2009), 8441, 8581.

4. *Merriam Webster's Collegiate Dictionary*, 562.

5. John Koessler, "2 Timothy," in *The Moody Bible Commentary*, Michael Rydelnik and Michael Vanlaningham, gen. eds. (Chicago: Moody, 2014), 1909.

6. "Strong's G217—halas," (ESV), Blue Letter Bible, https://www.blueletterbible .org/lexicon/g217/esv/mgnt/0-1/.

7. George Rawlinson, *The Kings of Israel and Judah* (London: James Nisbet and Co., 1899), 206.

8. C. Knapp, *Kings of Judah* (Dubuque, IA: ECS Ministries, 1909, revised 2004), 142.

9. Charles F. Pfeiffer, *Old Testament History* (Grand Rapids: Baker Book House, 1977), 370.

10. Lambert & Millarda/Catalogue of the cuneiform tablets in the Kouyujik Collection of the British Museum: Second Supplement Campbell Thompson 1931/The Prisms of Esarhaddon and of Ashurbanipal found at Nineveh 1927–8 (pp. 29–36, pls. 14–18) https://www.britishmuseum.org/collection/ object/W_1929-1012-2.

11. Pfeiffer, *Old Testament History*, 370.

12. *CSB Spurgeon Study Bible* (Nashville: Holman Bible Publishers, 2017), 1513.

13. Harry E. Shields, "2 Kings," in *The Moody Bible Commentary*, 548.

14. Yigal Levin, *The Chronicles of the Kings of Judah* (London: T&T Clark, 2017), 414.

15. Ibid.

16. Louis E. Newman, *Repentance: The Meaning and Practice of Teshuvah* (Woodstock, VT: Jewish Lights Publishing, 2010), 34, 76.

Week Eight: Remembering Heritage

1. "What Do Archaeologists Do?," Society for American Archaeology, https://www.saa.org/about-archaeology/what-do-archaeologists-do.
2. "Andrew Murray: Chapter XVIII: Entering the Covenant: With All the Heart," Blue Letter Bible, https://www.blueletterbible.org/Comm/murray_andrew/two/two18.cfm?a=336003.
3. Kari Jobe and Cody Carnes, "The Blessing," #4 Graves into Gardens, Elevation Worship, 2020.

Kings Genealogy Timeline with Prophets

1. Charts from Harry E. Shields, "1 Kings," in *The Moody Bible Commentary*, Michael Rydelnik and Michael Vanlaningham, gen. eds. (Chicago: Moody, 2014), 482–83.

Map of the Northern and Southern Kingdoms

1. Map from Barry J. Beitzel, *The New Moody Atlas of the Bible* (Chicago: Moody, 2009), 169.

Leader's Guide

1. "influencer," *Merriam-Webster.com Dictionary*, https://www.merriam-webster.com/dictionary/influencer.